BASIC GRAPHIC DESIGN & PASTE-UP

Jack Warren

BASIC GRAPHIC DESIGN & PASTE-UP

NORTH LIGHT PUBLISHERS

Published by North Light, an imprint
of F&W Publications, 1507 Dana
Avenue, Cincinnati, Ohio 45207.

Manufactured in U.S.A.
First Edition
First reprint, 1987

Library of Congress Cataloging-in-Publication Data

Warren, Jack, 1931—
    Basic graphic design and paste-up.

    Includes index.
    1. Printing, Practical—Layout.   2. Printing,
Practical—Paste-up techniques.   3. Graphic arts.
I. Title.
Z246.W36   1985   686.2′24   85-25913
ISBN 0-89134-127-7

"Trifles make perfection—and perfection is no trifle."
—Michelangelo, 1475–1564

Acknowledgments

I'd like to express my appreciation to all those who were so generous and helpful in allowing me to use examples of their work to illustrate this book.

Also, to Cor Videler of Saugatuck Photolab for his interest and contribution. And to my daughter Kim for transposing my chicken scratches into a readable manuscript. And finally to my wife, Kathi, who said I could do this when I said I didn't think I could, and put up with me when I did. My thanks to all.

Contents

Introduction

What Is a Graphic Designer?

In these days where specialization is a way of life, the term "commercial art" becomes a broad generalized label that fits just about any area of art or artist, from the serious easel painter who sells his work on a regular basis, or the illustrator whose work is commissioned, to the cartoonist whose work is either free-lanced or syndicated.

But there's another kind of artist—one who organizes words and pictures into a given area to make a clear, positive graphic statement. It may take the form of an advertisement, book jacket, package, record album cover, poster . . . virtually anything from a matchbook cover to a highway billboard. This proficient, versatile artist possesses a thorough working knowledge not only of all areas of art, but also photography, typography and reproduction methods. Such a person is a graphic designer. He or she is in every sense as much an artist as the painter, illustrator or cartoonist. Without question, many of the considerations required to create a successful picture are essential in producing a successful graphic design.

Graphic design—that's what this book is about. Before starting this project, I looked over the competition. There are several good books available, but they all have one common denominator: their presentation becomes so technical that it's frightening. Even though I understand what it is all about, reading it turns me off. This must be doubly true for the novice. An interested person with little knowledge of graphic design might well have second thoughts about getting involved in such a subject. And that's unfortunate, because graphic design can be a fascinating and rewarding occupation.

In presenting this material, I shall practice what I preach and show and tell my message in a clear, direct and straightforward manner. We'll leave the philosophy about the graphic designer's role in society, or the impact of their work in the marketplace, to those who wish to offer a different kind of message.

Someday, someone may ask you what you do for a living. When you tell them you're a graphic designer and they ask what that is, you can hold up your head and proudly say: "A graphic designer is an artist who organizes words and pictures into a given area to make a clear, positive, graphic statement."

And after you've told them that, you will no doubt get the same response I do: "Hey . . . Terrific! Can you make me a sign?"

Layout and Design

Understand Your Position

Make no mistake about it. When you elect to become a graphic designer, you elect to finish someone else's ideas. Your graphic effort, no matter what direction it may take—whether a newspaper ad, billboard, poster, package, whatever its form—will be directed toward selling or promoting a specific product or service. Someone else's, not yours. Your ultimate contribution will be a piece of work tailored and executed to reflect the conversations, instructions and agreements that have transpired between you and your client.

The Client

The client is the buyer of your work, the individual or organization who will pay you for your efforts. They have a message about their product or service that they wish to advertise or promote, and they have reached a point where they need your help.

What they have in mind when you meet may be definite or very vague. Either way, listen carefully; try to fully understand everything. If in doubt about something, ask questions.

Contribute ideas or suggestions if called upon, but be sure you both agree on just what is needed before you pick up the pencil and begin.

Your ultimate purpose is to convey a clear, direct graphic statement to a particular audience. You do this by establishing at the outset a forthright verbal communication with your client so you fully understand his needs. Such a dialogue is a most important preliminary stage of your assignment. All too often this initial step is left unresolved by both parties. To proceed with a project when everything is vague or unclear usually results in finished work that fails to fill the bill. No matter how carefully done, such work

This poster by Henri Toulouse-Lautrec (1864-1901) is an excellent example of graphic design. His use of bold, arresting shapes produces a clear, direct graphic statement. The same principles are used today to create a quality of graphic design that rises well above most advertising.

13

will require extensive changes or a complete redo. How sad—all that time and effort down the drain. Avoid the waste by getting all the facts before you start.

Clear communication is particularly important when working with an advertising agency, studio or design department of a company. You'll then be part of a team and you may have little or no direct contact with the client.

Your information about the job at hand may come to you from an account executive, an art director or some other individual who deals with the source and passes information on to you. Be careful. This is like telling a joke or story to someone who repeats it to others. It goes around in a conversational circle, and about a week later it gets back to you. In its altered form you hardly recognize it as your original story. Something changed or was lost in the transmission. So check and double-check all information connected with your assignment before you begin. Make sure you get the right story. It will save you a lot of grief later.

Recognize Your Limitations
Telling you to recognize your limitations should in no way suggest a restriction be put on your imagination. The limits of your creativity will be of your doing, not mine. Don't impose any. Bring to each job, no matter how large or small, the broadest possible thought.

The limitations I'm referring to relate to time, money and space. Usually one or more of these factors will apply to any job you do. In most cases all three are of prime concern.

And they should be. The nature of the business and the real world requires you to deal with these facts of life and come up with some

answers—not only for yourself, but for your client. Typical of the questions that will arise when discussing a job will be: "What will this cost? How long will it take? Does it have to be that big?"

On the other hand, your client may already have these answers and will inform you up front exactly how much is to be spent on the job and when it is needed—the *deadline*. Whether the deadline is realistic or impossible, it goes with the territory. Get used to it. Finally, you may be told just what size space with which you have to work. This may leave you with the feeling of having to fit a two-pound package into a one-pound bag.

Once you understand these factors, you'll have a better idea of the direction and approach the job requires. Regardless of the limitations, whether they be reasonable or not, they should not put a restriction on the quality of thought and craftsman-ship you use to execute the job. Limitations are part of every job. As a graphic designer, you must learn to live with them. Give each job your best effort, and you'll never have reason to justify or apologize for what you've done.

Graphic design takes many directions and can be applied to virtually any subject. When done with thought and care it can greatly enhance any product or service. The clear, direct approach as shown in Lautrec's work is always in style. The above examples reflect the result of this kind of thinking.

Basic Elements of a Design

A great deal has been written about artistic creativity. Some of it makes sense, some of it is rather foolish. The more I study the subject, the more I am convinced the graphic artist is best served by thinking in terms of *common sense* and *organization*. The ability to apply common sense and organize a graphic problem is the best way I have found to get positive results.

There are three basic elements to be dealt with as you begin your assignment. They are: Illustration, Type and Signature.

Illustration will be the word used here to define a drawing, painting, photograph or any graphic symbol that illustrates.

Type or *typography* (which will be detailed more fully in Section 2) refers to the copy, text, manuscript, or more simply, the words. As a graphic designer, part of your job is to make these words visual. This requires space in your design and must be given that consideration.

The *signature* identifies the person, persons, or company responsible for the message your graphics project.

Sometimes the signature is simply set in type. Often it is a graphic design in itself that has been carefully thought out and executed. It usually reflects the quality of product or service being offered and can be found not only on all printed material, but in many cases is also engraved or stamped on the product itself if one is involved. This is known as one's *Trademark*, sometimes referred to as the logo.

TYPOGRAPHY

To begin with, the design of a piece of printing should be considered in its relation to the idea of the thing itself, its sale and use. Obviously, the type faces, color scheme and illustration should be keyed to the end of making it easy for the reader to get the idea of the advertiser, for results are what count. Type should therefore be employed with proper consideration for its force in presenting the copy

Illustration—Type—Signature. These are the key elements that constantly challenge the graphic designer. They must be designed to fit into a given area in such a way that they work in harmony with each other to produce a clear, graphic statement. As we work with these elements on the following pages, the approach will be one of common sense and good judgement rather than the application of hard-and-fast rules.

Getting Underway

The meetings, discussions, brainstorming and masterminding sessions are over. Everyone concerned is now focusing on you to translate all this input into a clear, direct, graphic statement.

Where to start?

Begin by reading the copy. Don't just look at it and wonder how much space it will take. Read it—more than once—and try to understand what has been written. You'd be surprised just how many times this can produce a clue or an idea of what kind of direction might be taken. I never cease to be amazed at the number of designers, amateur and pro alike, who look upon the written word as just another design element to contend with, giving little concern as to its content.

Visualizing the Approach

Shown here are some abstract diagrams suggesting the three basic elements—illustration, type and signature. These sketches show how the elements can be designed within a standard space of 8½x11 inches (the size of this page). You'll be surprised as you advance in your career just how many times this format will become your arena. Sooner or later almost everything happening in the world gets recorded within its boundaries.

Figure 1 shows our elements as they might look with all things being equal, that is, illustration and type occupying the same amount of space. It usually doesn't end up this way, and if it does, the result tends to be rather static.

Figure 2 shows how the design might work if the copy were short, requiring little room when set in a legible type. This gives us the opportunity to play up the illustration

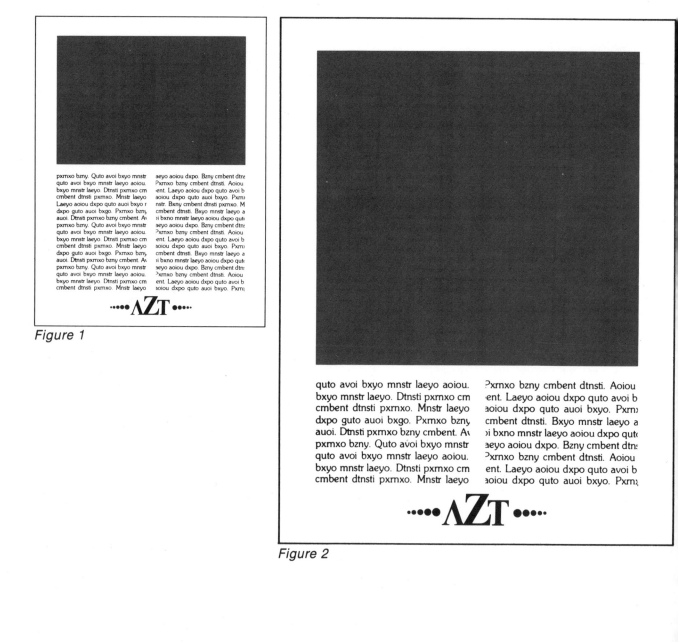

Figure 1

Figure 2

to its best advantage. This layout is likely to have more interest.

Conversely, Figure 3 shows what would happen if the copy, again set in a legible type, runs quite deep and requires a large area of the page. We still have the illustration to consider. The answer would be to scale the picture down in size or crop out all but the essentials (these procedures will be detailed in Section 3). Most designers are reluctant to cut down on the illustration. They believe the old Chinese saying that a picture is worth a thousand words. Clients, however, may not agree. They may feel that lengthy prose is the way to go, and since they're paying the freight, that is likely to end the argument.

Laeyo aoiou dxpo quto auoi bxyo r
dxpo guto auoi bxgo. Pxrnxo bzny
auoi. Dtnsti pxrnxo bzny cmbent. Av
pxrnxo bzny. Quto avoi bxyo mnstr
quto avoi bxyo mnstr laeyo aoiou.
bxyo mnstr laeyo. Dtnsti pxrnxo cm
cmbent dtnsti pxrnxo. Mnstr laeyo
dxpo guto auoi bxgo. Pxrnxo bzny
auoi. Dtnsti pxrnxo bzny cmbent. Av
pxrnxo bzny. Quto avoi bxyo mnstr
quto avoi bxyo mnstr laeyo aoiou.
bxyo mnstr laeyo. Dtnsti pxrnxo cm
cmbent dtnsti pxrnxo. Mnstr laeyo
Laeyo aoiou dxpo quto auoi bxyo r
dxpo guto auoi bxgo. Pxrnxo bzny
auoi. Dtnsti pxrnxo bzny cmbent. Av
pxrnxo bzny. Quto avoi bxyo mnstr
quto avoi bxyo mnstr laeyo aoiou.
bxyo mnstr laeyo. Dtnsti pxrnxo cm
cmbent dtnsti pxrnxo. Mnstr laeyo
dxpo guto auoi bxgo. Pxrnxo bzny
auoi. Dtnsti pxrnxo bzny cmbent. Av
pxrnxo bzny. Quto avoi bxyo mnstr
quto avoi bxyo mnstr laeyo aoiou.
bxyo mnstr laeyo. Dtnsti pxrnxo cm
cmbent dtnsti pxrnxo. Mnstr laeyo

nstr. Bxny cmbent dtnsti pxrnxo. M
cmbent dtnsti. Bxyo mnstr laeyo a
ɔi bxno mnstr laeyo aoiou dxpo qutɔ
aeyo aoiou dxpo. Bzny cmbent dtns
Pxrnxo bzny cmbent dtnsti. Aoiou
ent. Laeyo aoiou dxpo quto avoi b
aoiou dxpo quto auoi bxyo. Pxrnɔ
cmbent dtnsti. Bxyo mnstr laeyo a
ɔi bxno mnstr laeyo aoiou dxpo qutɔ
aeyo aoiou dxpo. Bzny cmbent dtns
Pxrnxo bzny cmbent dtnsti. Aoiou
ent. Laeyo aoiou dxpo quto avoi b
aoiou dxpo quto auoi bxyo. Pxrnɔ
nstr. Bxny cmbent dtnsti pxrnxo. M
cmbent dtnsti. Bxyo mnstr laeyo a
ɔi bxno mnstr laeyo aoiou dxpo qutɔ
aeyo aoiou dxpo. Bzny cmbent dtns
Pxrnxo bzny cmbent dtnsti. Aoiou
ent. Laeyo aoiou dxpo quto avoi b
aoiou dxpo quto auoi bxyo. Pxrnɔ
cmbent dtnsti. Bxyo mnstr laeyo a
ɔi bxno mnstr laeyo aoiou dxpo qutɔ
aeyo aoiou dxpo. Bzny cmbent dtn:
Pxrnxo bzny cmbent dtnsti. Aoiou
ent. Laeyo aoiou dxpo quto avoi b
aoiou dxpo quto auoi bxyo. Pxrnɔ

Figure 3

Although this example most closely follows Figure 2 on the preceding page, there is no rule that dictates the illustration, type and signature must be shown in this sequence. The other examples demonstrate an entirely different approach in using these elements in the same given area. The problem was the same but the results are varied. Take the time and effort needed to explore the possible ways the elements you are working with can be designed for optimum effect.

Courtesy Scents & Such

Long Wharf Maritime Center
Gateway To New England

Corporate Offices • Shops • Marina • Restaurants • Parking Facilities • Hotel

New England's most accessible and picturesque harbor frontage is about to become New Haven's Showplace Business Center.

Long Wharf, New Haven Harbor at Interstates 91 and 95. Occupancy 1985. 220,000 square feet available.

The Southern New England Telephone Company was first to reserve 210,000 square feet for its engineering headquarters. Join them at the Long Wharf Maritime Center.

For leasing information call:
FUSCO CORPORATION
777-7451
142 Temple Street
New Haven, CT

Office Park Garage | Office Building III Shops, Restaurants | Waterfront Promenade | Office Building II | Office Building I

ATRIUM BUILDING I

CURE 81®
Registered lean, tender and naturally smoked.

Hormel America's first name for ham.

Advertising that has much to say but little to illustrate can be a boring visual experience. There is much of it around, so don't add to it. Organize and present your elements in the best possible manner. Consider the weight, size and "color" of the type (so called, although it is usually gray) as an important part of the design. We'll take a closer look at type and how it works in Section 2. The examples here show what a clear, direct, well-thought-out approach can produce.

Seated, l. to r.: Bennett Cerf, Faith Baldwin, Bergen Evans, Bruce Catton, Mignon G. Eberhart, John Caples, J. D. Ratcliff. Standing: Mark Wiseman, Max Shulman, Rudolf Flesch, Red Smith, Rod Serling.

Photo: Halsman

"We're looking for people who want to write"

If you want to write and see your work published, here's an opportunity never before available:

Twelve of America's most famous authors have created a school of professional writing to help you develop your skill, talent and craftsmanship . . . and to pass on to you their secrets of achieving success and recognition.

They include Rod Serling, winner of five TV Emmys; best-selling novelist Faith Baldwin; Pulitzer Prize historian Bruce Catton; humorist Max Shulman; publisher-columnist Bennett Cerf.

Over a three-year period, they developed home-study courses in Fiction, Non-Fiction, Advertising and Business Writing. (The first three contain sections on TV writing.) They poured into a series of textbooks and writing assignments everything they had learned in their long, hard climb to the top.

When you return an assignment to the School, one of the instructors—who are all professional writers—spends up to two hours analyzing your work. He blue-pencils corrections on your manuscript, much as an editor does with established authors. And he returns it with a long letter of specific recommendations on how to improve your writing.

The School is young. Yet students, most of them still in training, have sold their work to over 60 different publications, including *Reader's Digest, Redbook, Popular Science.*

"My first article sold to *Better Homes and Gardens!*" exults Mrs. Lillian Maas. "I've just sold a story to *True* for $1,000," reports Alfred Gaumer, "and I owe it all to your training."

Writing-aptitude test offered

To find other people with writing ability worth developing, the 12 famous writers have created a revealing Aptitude Test. The postpaid reply card on the next page will bring you a copy, along with a 48-page School brochure.

Your completed test will be graded and returned without charge by one of the School's instructors. If you show aptitude, you are eligible to enroll in the School. However, there is no obligation to do so. (To get your test if reply card is missing, send name, address, age to Famous Writers School, Dept. 6477, Westport, Conn.)

Courtesy Famous Writers Schools

O'NEILL AT MIDTERM:
HOW'S HE DOING?

BY NED BARNETT

BIL-LEE, BIL-LEE, BIL-LEE," arose the chant of welcome as William Atchison O'Neill entered the ornate hall of the House on January 5, 1983. As O'Neill, smiling and waving, mounted the speaker's dais to face the crowd of representatives, senators and dignitaries, polite applause faded beneath the sound of a deep, robust intonation: "Yoooooooo.... Yoooooooo..., Yoooooooo...."

The chanting of a nickname and the whooping tribal tone contrasted with the Victorian decorum of the lower chamber and the weightiness of the occasion: O'Neill's inauguration as governor in his own right. Yet if the raucous greeting seemed more appropriate for a Saturday night in O'Neill's East Hampton taproom, so also was it fitting here. For the friends that raised the exuberant ruckus—friends first made as colleagues during O'Neill's 12 years in the House—were there not merely to see a new governor set forth; they were there to welcome back a buddy, a dear and loyal friend for whom that day of commencement also marked the end of one of the more poignant

"BIL-LEE, BIL-LEE, BIL-LEE..."

political journeys in Connecticut history.

It was a journey O'Neill had not chosen to undertake, and one that he and many others had doubted his ability to complete. For when that journey began, O'Neill was a

51-year-old lieutenant governor who had never demonstrated the ambition or the mettle required of those who traverse uncharted political paths. True, he had at that point already made progress in state politics. From the post he had assumed in 1966 as state representative from his lifelong home of East Hampton, he had risen upward to House majority leader, to Democratic state party chairman and finally, in 1978, he assumed the office of lieutenant governor. That progress had been achieved by plodding down the middle of the road, carefully avoiding points of controversy and dissent. And no matter how far he traveled, he never left behind the image of the man he was at the beginning: a conservative, rural politician without a college education who made his living tending the tavern he had inherited from his father.

On New Year's Eve 1980, when barkeepers throughout the world were surrounded by jubilation, O'Neill found himself in the midst of gloom. Gov. Ella Grasso, diagnosed as terminally ill with cancer and soon to die, had resigned her office on December 31, leaving Bill O'Neill to govern without preparation, without a mandate and, in many

Most politicians and voters agree that the governor is doing a better job than anyone expected when he came to office. But that kind of praise may not be enough to win him the vote in '86.

JANUARY 1985 CONNECTICUT 51

Courtesy Connecticut Magazine

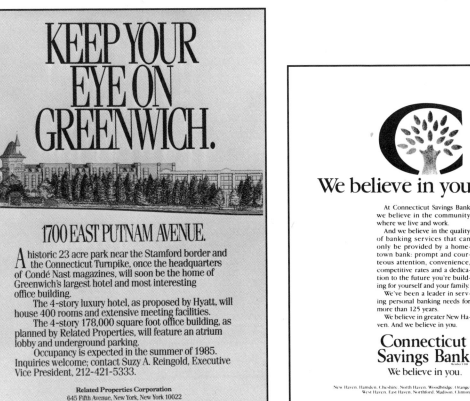

KEEP YOUR EYE ON GREENWICH.

1700 EAST PUTNAM AVENUE.

A historic 23 acre park near the Stamford border and the Connecticut Turnpike, once the headquarters of Condé Nast magazines, will soon be the home of Greenwich's largest hotel and most interesting office building.

The 4-story luxury hotel, as proposed by Hyatt, will house 400 rooms and extensive meeting facilities.

The 4-story 178,000 square foot office building, as planned by Related Properties, will feature an atrium lobby and underground parking.

Occupancy is expected in the summer of 1985. Inquiries welcome; contact Suzy A. Reingold, Executive Vice President, 212-421-5333.

Related Properties Corporation
645 Fifth Avenue, New York, New York 10022

Courtesy Related Properties Corporation

We believe in you.

At Connecticut Savings Bank we believe in the community where we live and work.

And we believe in the quality of banking services that can only be provided by a hometown bank: prompt and courteous attention, convenience, competitive rates and a dedication to the future you're building for yourself and your family.

We've been a leader in serving personal banking needs for more than 125 years.

We believe in greater New Haven. And we believe in you.

Connecticut Savings Bank
Member FDIC
We believe in you.

New Haven, Hamden, Cheshire, North Haven, Woodbridge, Orange, West Haven, East Haven, Northford, Madison, Clinton

Courtesy Connecticut Savings Bank

Lease or buy? Edart opens a loophole.

AN ADVANTAGE YOU CAN TAKE TO THE BANK.

Up to now, some of the financial advantages of buying a fleet of trucks outweighed the benefits of leasing. But at Edart, we're evening the odds. As Connecticut's largest independent truck leasing firm, we've beefed up our leasing programs to deliver the kinds of bonuses you can add directly to your bottom line.

It's not our ITC. It's yours.
Right from the start, we'll make leasing pay. By passing on 100% of the Investment Tax Credit we get as the lessor. It's money you used to have to "own" in order to get. And that's just the beginning.

Truck leasing frees up assets you'd be tying up in expensive equipment and maintenance facilities. Leasing from Edart frees working capital for expansion or building inventory.

And consider how leasing improves cash management and accounting systems: your transportation costs are fixed up front, allowing more accurate forecasts. More reliable budgets. More realistic pricing.

The trucks you need.
When you need them.
Once a free Edart transportation analysis establishes what your fleet

needs are, we'll design a program to keep you going at 100% capacity 100% of the time. With extra trucks during peak shipping periods. **Free replacements** for trucks down for repairs. And a commitment to service that will never leave you stuck without a truck.

On the road again.
We're a member of the NationaLease system, a network of 200 independent leasing companies throughout North America. By pooling our resources we can ensure prompt, expert breakdown service seven days a week. Twenty-four hours a day. From Ogunquit to Oakland.

It's what makes the term **full-service leasing** a way of doing business rather than just a slogan.

Guaranteed truck availability. Round the clock service. Attention to detail. These are the reasons we're certain we can make leasing from Edart pay. From the biggest transportation problem to the smallest detail in paperwork it takes to keep your products on the move, we take care of it all.

Make us prove it.
More and more companies

are finding that leasing affords substantial savings in time, money headaches compared with fleet ownership or contracting.

Find out why. In a brochure that begins to put our promise in the language of fleet facts and figures. Ask about a free analysis of your transportation picture that can help you decide between owning and leasing. To get a copy, call the toll-free number.

We wrote the book on leasing and making it pay.

And we'll pass on the Investment Tax Credit the minute you get behind the wheel.

Free Fleet facts phone:
(in Conn.)
1-800-842-0026
(outside Conn.)
1-800-243-8992.

EDART
The driving force in leasing

Corporate Headquarters

Hartford, CT	North Haven, CT	Ayer, MA
185 West Service Road	37 Nettleton Avenue	2 Westford Road
Bridgeport, CT	Waterbury, CT	Wayne, NJ
376 Howard Avenue	106 Reidville Drive	2358 Hamburg Turnpike

Courtesy Edart Corporation

23

Working with Multiple Elements

Many times you will be working with several illustrations accompanied by a great deal of copy. What to do? This is when the two-pounds-in-the-one-pound-bag feeling begins to creep over you. But let's give it some thought and apply a common-sense approach.

The copy, as you have it, is probably in its final edited form, so the space it will occupy when set in type at a legible size will determine the amount of space left for illustration.

Figure 4 shows what might happen using three illustrations and type. It all fits, but as in Figure 1, the result looks static and uninteresting. To create interest we need variety. Let's keep that thought in mind as we proceed—*variety creates interest.*

Figure 5 demonstrates this. By varying the size of each illustration, even though they occupy the same area as in Figure 4, we have created a more pleasing, exciting design. By playing up one of the three illustrations, you create a *visual hook.* If the viewers find interest in the one large illustration, they will probably follow through by viewing the other two, then reading the copy. If this happens, you've done

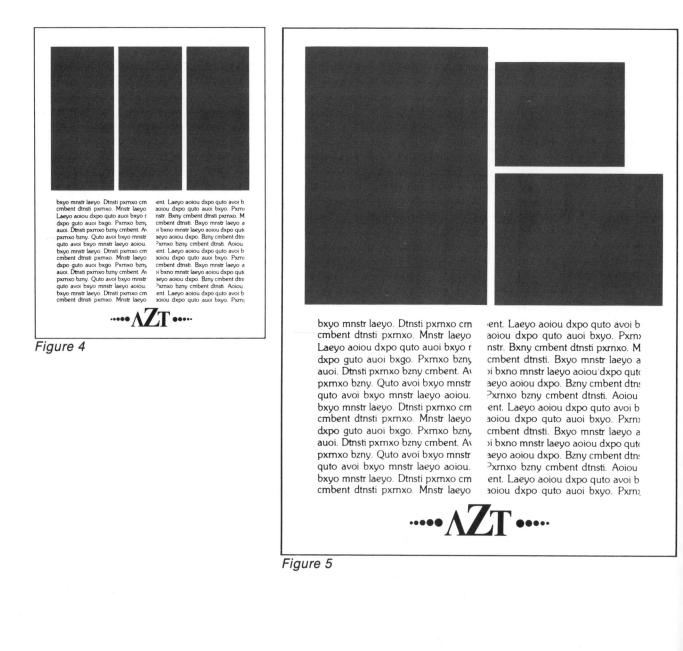

Figure 4

Figure 5

24

your job well.

This principle of *variety creates interest* is especially true in poster design, where you have about five seconds to attract the viewer's attention. The posters of Toulouse-Lautrec are an excellent example of this. He learned early how to create variety and interest through clear, bold, direct graphics.

Figures 6 and 7 are variations of the same theme. Notice in Figure 6 how interest is further achieved by having the copy set in a "flush left, ragged right" format as opposed to a copy block that has been "justified"—squared up on both sides. This creates a pleasing contrast to the straight edges of the illustrations. It also allows for consistent spacing between the typeset words—a condition not often possible in a justified line.

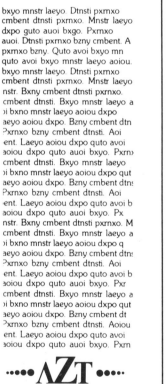

Figure 6

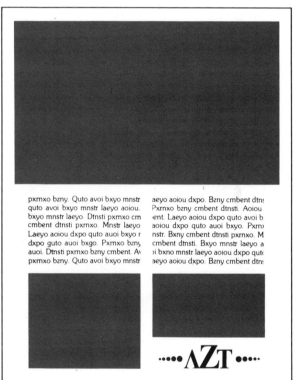

Figure 7

25

These examples demonstrate the use of variety to create interest. They play up the visual hook to draw your attention to their message. Were all the illustrations one size or shape and placed one next to another, the result would surely have been an overcrowded, monotonous look that would have conveyed little excitement to the viewer.

Courtesy Westport Bank & Trust

Culbro Land Resources, Incorporated

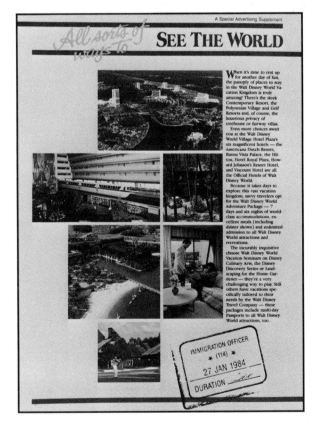
27

Unusual Shapes or Areas

Many times you will be faced with developing a design within an unusual area such as a square, circle or a rectangle of extreme proportions. At first glance such a situation might be alarming, but don't let it throw you. There is usually a workable solution. Carefully study the elements and the area to discover a way that they can complement each other.

First in **AM STEREO**

1st in 1AM STEREO

BIG BANDS SWING

Using Type as the Only Element of Design

There will be many cases where you will be working with no illustrative material at all, just copy. The problem here is to make the verbal elements visual . . . and interesting. Copy simply transposed to type, no matter how handsome or elegant the face, can still be a boring sight unless you create a *visual hook* to make your viewer take notice. Once again—start by reading the copy! Whether it be one word, a paragraph or a page, look for some way to establish variety and interest.

FOR 165 YEARS, WE'VE LOOKED AFTER YOUR SAVINGS. NOW, WE'RE LOOKING FOR YOUR TRUST.

Society, the bank that has always been known for quality banking services, combined with close personal attention, now offers complete trust, estate and financial planning services, as well as tax and employee benefit services for business—all at highly competitive fees.

In today's highly charged and rapidly changing economic environment, financial planning has become increasingly more important to practically everyone who earns an income and holds investments or property worth protecting. That's why Society's unique approach to this complicated and often intimidating subject is welcome news to so many Society customers and Connecticut people.

We've combined the latest techniques in financial planning and asset management with Society's long tradition of personal attention, to create a friendly, professional environment. With patience (and in plain English), we'll work with you and your attorney or accountant to inventory and analyze your assets, and structure them for more effective management and minimum tax impact.

With 14 years experience advising people on trust and investment matters, Charlie Hanscomb and Don Wilmot are the people you'll want to speak with at Society's Investment Services/Trust Department.

SOCIETY'S ON THE MOVE

Society for Savings, Member FDIC

Courtesy Society for Savings

THE VARIETY OF EXCELLENCE.

There are more than 50 Westin Hotels worldwide. Each is as unique as the city or the nation it serves.

Yet there is a similarity of character. A feeling of quality. In our guest rooms, in our cuisine, in our meeting facilities. Plus a level of personal service and attention to detail that makes you feel you are the most important person in the hotel. And indeed you are.

As our guest, we believe you should expect one standard in all things.

Excellence.

ALL ELSE PASSES BUT ART ALONE ENDURES THE BUST OUTLASTS THE THRONE · THE COIN TIBERIUS

ART has its own position in industry and it need not necessarily be what is known as commercial art; it need only be art. When business men thoroughly learn that art can be itself and still be useful to them; when they cease distorting it in the effort to adapt it to business; then only will they realize its full commercial value. Let the artist remain an artist and the business man a business man; but let them understand each other thoroughly and always work together in harmony. Art will then take its rightful place in American life as a useful factor in all things worth while; as an ally of business in advertising and in the designing of products advertised; and business is almost sure to profit from the partnership

The Corporate Image

Here's a fascinating area of graphic design. Its origin is as old as the beginnings of business and commerce . . . from the unique and highly original signboards displayed by the early European and American inns and pubs to the names and initials that were carved or scratched into the handmade products wrought by proud craftsmen. It was their mark of trade—their trademark. It's still very much with us today. As mentioned earlier, the signature or trademark is an integral part of most design projects, and in many cases it is a well-conceived graphic design in itself.

Companies of all types and sizes have been known to spend huge sums of money and devote much time and effort to acquire that certain look they wish to convey to the public. Everyone from the president's wife to the secretary's assistant may get involved, but when all the masterminding is over and the dust settles, it's the graphic designer they finally turn to for the expertise needed to bring to final visual form what they can only talk about.

A company's corporate image includes not only the logo but also its

Courtesy Fusco Corporation

Courtesy North American Bank

Courtesy Westport Broadcasting Company, Incorporated

32

use—on stationery, invoices, labels, architectural signage, publications, company vehicles, uniforms, products and advertising. A particular combination of colors is often involved. But the logo (short for "logotype") is central to the plan.

Designing the signature, trademark or logo can be a challenging and exciting project. Don't be misled by the apparent simplicity of these designs.

They are the result of much concentrated thinking, research and thought.

The result in many cases becomes a design of remarkable permanence. Some of the designs shown here were done many years ago but are still much in evidence today. The potential longevity of a trademark's existence dictates an approach of simplicity and clarity.

Courtesy RCA Corporation

CELANESE

Courtesy Celanese Corporation

EASTERN

Courtesy Eastern Airlines

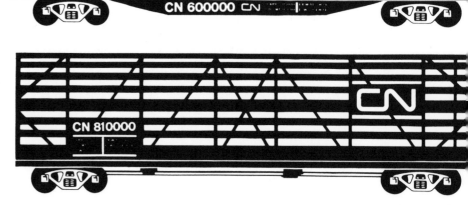

CN

Here's an example of the trademark at work. Canadian National Railways graphically demonstrates how their logo is used on passenger and freight equipment as well as directional and information signs, even to its business forms, stationery, interior decor. A well-designed trademark works on anything—from a locomotive to a calling card.

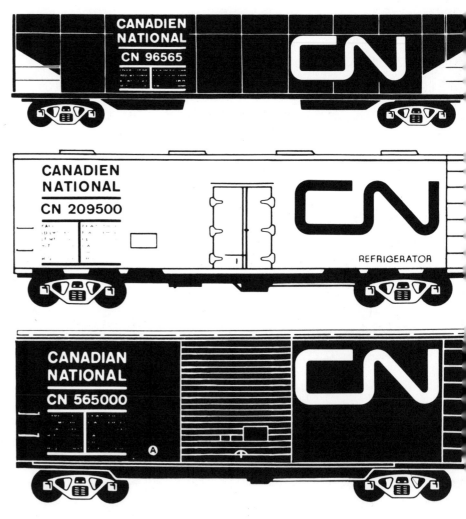

Courtesy Canadian National Railways

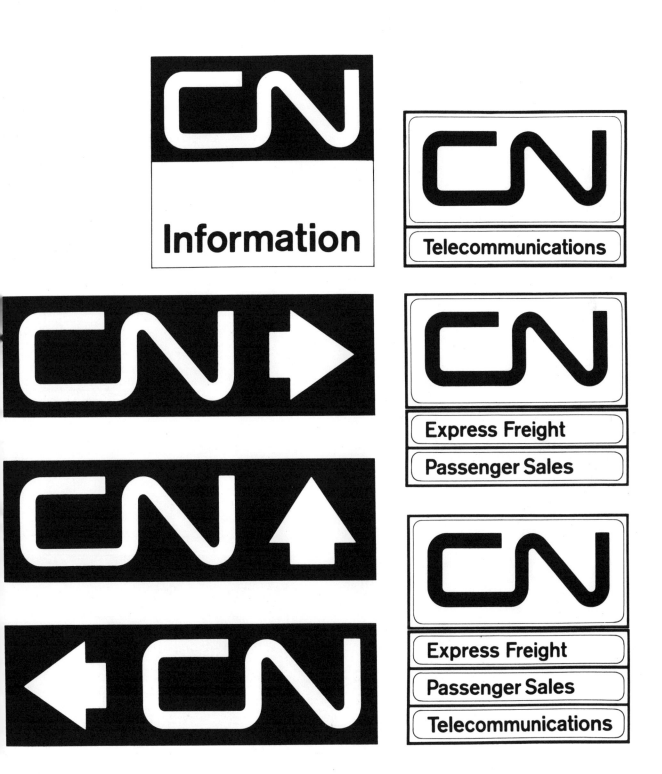

Sources for Art and Design

More often than not what your client would like to see in the way of illustration and design is not in keeping with what he is willing to spend for it. This is called working on a "Limited Budget." Translation: "Think big . . . but cheap."

Don't let this situation, which happens with great regularity, discourage you. There are ways to work within the limited budget and still produce a quality job. Sources known as "clip art services" can supply you, at modest cost, with a collection of art on virtually any subject you may need. Once you buy it, it's yours, to use over again as much as you like. There are also agencies that can supply stock

photographs on any subject. Fees for one-time use of the pictures are often on a sliding scale based on your project's budget or publication circulation. There are books to be had that contain fine old engravings that, because of their age, have come into the public domain. This means they are copyright free and anyone may reproduce them. (However, if the work of art you wish to use is privately owned, you must get the owner's written permission to publish it. This usually requires the payment of a fee.)

Listed here are a few of several sources where this material can be found. I'm sure that further investigation on your part can turn up

Here are some examples of ready-to-use art chosen at random from the Volk Clip Art collection. As you can see, the styles vary in their approach and the subject matter is endless. If you wish further information, the clip art services listed can supply you with catalogs as to what they have to offer.

others. Two good places to start would be your local library and art supply store.

Volk Clip Art
P.O. Box 72
Pleasantville, NJ 08232

Formost Clip Art
Graphic Products Corporation
3601 Edison Place
Rolling Meadows, IL 60008

Dynamic Graphics, Incorporated
Clipper Creative Art Service
Peoria, IL 61614

Need a halloween witch? Take your choice. Realistic, humorous or stylized, ready-to-use clip art like this can often be the answer to the making of an interesting design. Its cost is moderate; it enables you to turn out a professional-looking job while still working within the confines of the "limited budget."

Here is a sampling of some beautiful old engravings chosen from The Handbook of Early Advertising Art offered by Dover Publications. Because of their age, they have come into the public domain. That means they're copyright free and you may reproduce them in virtually any way you wish. The collection in this book offers a wide range of style and subject matter. Many an uninspired design has been raised to classic elegance by the addition of one of these fine pieces of old art. Dover offers many books on art, engravings and woodcuts. For information write to:

Dover Publications, Incorporated
Department DA
180 Varick Street
New York, NY 10014

38

Typography

Then and Now

One of my first jobs in graphic design was to lay out an ad for a newspaper, indicating the area for type. The production man criticized my efforts by saying that what I did wouldn't work, that I was approaching typography as if it were "as flexible as rubber." I wish he were here today to tell me that.

Typography, long regarded as a field dominated by master craftsmen who earned their trade from the ground up through years of apprenticeship, has, in every sense of the word, become a graphic example of what happens when technology takes over.

Type has progressed from setting each letter, word and line laboriously by hand, to the Linotype machine, which did it faster and better mechanically, to its present day state of the art known as computerized photocomposition. This makes what was once impossible, a common everyday occurrence. You can now have type set not only in any size you desire, but you can have it slanted right or left, condensed, expanded, set straight or in a circle—just about any way you specify.

Computerized phototypography, over the last few years, has completely altered the typesetting industry, spawning a myriad of one- or two-person basement or garage typographic services. The large type houses have adapted (some reluctantly) to the computer age in order to survive.

What they have to offer in the way of type is mind boggling. To sell their services, many will give you 2x3-foot posters showing at least a hundred typefaces that you can hang on the wall for reference. If that's not enough, they have even more faces catalogued in books so thick and elaborate you can't help but wonder where to begin.

There are only three styles of type.

Any typeface you've ever seen or ever will see is based on one of three basic styles—roman, gothic or script. There are, of course, almost unlimited variations within each of these categories.

A roman style is sometimes referred to as a serif typeface because of the way it flares out at the top, bottom or end of the letter form.

A gothic style is sometimes called a

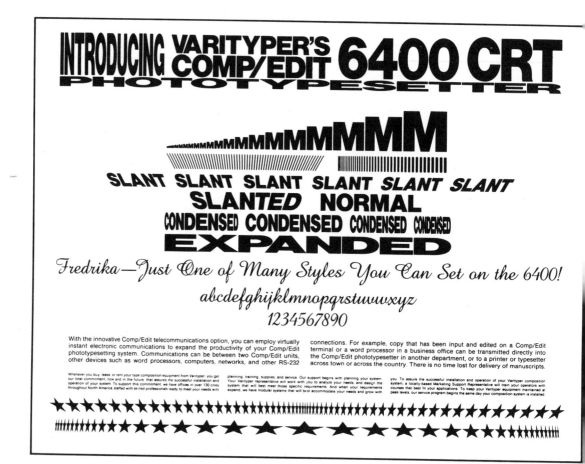

ans-serif typeface. *Sans* means
without, and that's just what it is, a
clean letter form with sharp, clean
ends.

Script needs little definition. As you
can see by the example, it appears to
be a very refined version of
handwriting. Some styles have more
flourish than others, but any letter that
connects to another, whether straight
up or slanted, formal or casual, usually
falls into the category of script.

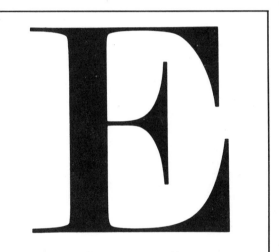

Roman or serif

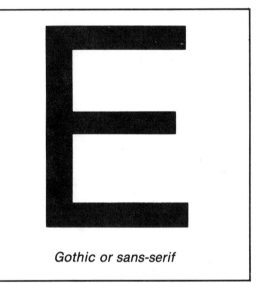

Gothic or sans-serif

Script

Typography grows on you. Your appreciation for it doesn't happen overnight. It occurs over a period of time, and for some designers, it becomes a lasting love affair. Some choose to specialize in nothing but design and use of typography.

As you become more aware of type, you will start to notice that in the mountain of printed material which is a daily part of your life, certain pieces stand out above the others. Their quality is readily apparent. Investigation will show that their exceptional look is partly the result of the use of only one or two well-chosen typefaces.

A good example of this is the book you are now reading. The entire text has been set in a typeface called Helvetica. It was chosen for its excellent variety. It not only has a complete alphabet of capital and lowercase letters including figures and punctuation marks (all this is known as a *font* of type), but it also offers the variations of size, italic, bold, extended and condensed. (This is called a *family*

Although the selection of typefaces that are available may seem endless and confusing, bear in mind that all the typefaces you will find are but variations of the three types shown above. The column of faces on the left fall into the Roman, or serif category, while the center column is a variation of Gothic, or sans serif, and the column on the right reflects a few versions of script. As you develop a keener eye for type you will be able to more easily identify, clarify and classify the typefaces you come across.

Antique Bold

Argos Semibold

AUGUSTEA INLINE

Benguait Book

Benguait Medium

Benguait Bold

Bernhard Modern Bold

BETON OPEN

Bookman Bold Italic

BROKER

BROKER SHADED

Carnaby

Caslon No. 540

Caslon Black Swash

Caslon Old Style 37E

Caslon Openface

Century Expanded

of type.) It works well for this book because it can be used for everything from headline or display, subheads, body (what you are now reading), to captions—right down to a footnote.

There is no hard, fast rule about using just one typeface for any given job. There's no limit. But you will find, as your awareness grows, that you seldom need more than two. Beyond that, the job begins to lose its clarity. Just because you have something to say doesn't mean you have to use every available typeface to do it. Simplicity denotes quality—and that's what you're after.

The study of typefaces will grow on you. It is a marvelously complex subject. In time you'll gain appreciation and knowledge that this or any other book can't possibly provide. What follows are guidelines and examples to give you an approach. Only experience, trial and error, and a healthy curiousity about what you are doing will lead you to your own evaluation of what is excellent in this fascinating area of graphic design.

Adonis Extended

Adonis Extended ITALIC

Alternate Gothic No. 2

Alternate Gothic No. 2 Italic

Aurora Bold Condensed

AUTOMATION

Avant Garde Gothic X-LIGHT

Avant Garde Gothic MEDIUM

Avant Garde Gothic BOLD

Benguait Gothic Book

Benguait Gothic Medium

Benguait Gothic Bold

Bolt Bold

BUSORAMA BOLD

BUXOM

Chalk

CHARTER OAK

Commercial Script

Dandy

Decor

Delight

Diana Script Light

Diana Script Bold

Diane Jeanine

Engravers Old English

Fresh

Friar

Gale

Gaston

Gillies Gothic Light

Gillies Gothic Bold

Gong

Grace

Invitation

Type Lingo — A Language All Its Own

Although the metric system has been gaining popularity in the United States in recent years, many measurements in terms of inches, feet, yards, etc., are still common. Type size is measured in points. Not being a whiz at mathematics, everything I've ever read about measuring type has confused me. With that in mind, I am going to convey this as simply and directly as possible.

Type is measured in points, not inches or centimeters. Here are some of the equivalent measurements involved:

- 72 points equals 1 inch, or 2.54 cm.
- 12 points equals 1 pica or .423 cm.
- 6 picas equals 1 inch, or 2.54 cm.
- The height of type is measured in points.
- The width of type set in a line (such as the one you are now reading) is measured in picas.*

Using what you are now reading as an example, you are looking at text that has been set in 10 point type, in a flush left, ragged right format, with the longest line being 14 picas wide. Using the inch for comparison, this means

Characters

ROMAN ae — Bodoni   ae — Caslon Oldstyle   ae — Century Oldstyle

GOTHIC ae — Helvetica   ae — Lydian   ae — Optima

Character Variations within the Roman and Gothic Styles

* The point sizes referred to here are used only in English-speaking countries. The Swiss, Germans and French, among others, have different type measuring systems.

hat this type is $^{10}/_{72}$ of an inch high nd it runs 2$^1/_3$ inches in width.

The height of any typeface is neasured from its highest capital or owercase ascender to the bottom of s lowest descender. (See illustration.)

There is a special vocabulary used vhen dealing with type. Some of the nore common terms are listed here.

Font. Complete alphabet of capital nd lowercase letters, including figures nd punctuation marks.

Character. This refers to an ndividual letter, figure or punctuation nark, or a space between words or unctuation marks.

Rules. A line in typography. Such nes can be used for everything from

Height of Type

ABCDEFGH
IJKLMNOP
QRSTUVW
XYZ &?!ß£$
abcdefghijk
lmnopqrstu
vwxyz12345
67890();⁰⁄₀≋

A Font of Type

Here is what is called a family of type. Each font is a variation of the typeface Helvetica, the same face used throughout this book. As you can see, there is great variety here. The choices range from light to medium to bold, extra bold, condensed, extended and italic. There are several other typefaces, both Gothic and Roman, that offer this same range. As stated in Section 1, "variety creates interest." Here's a way to achieve it without resorting to the use of different and unrelated typefaces that add little but confusion to a design.

HELVETICA BOLD

HELVETICA LIGHT

HELVETICA LIGHT CONDENSED

ABCDEFGHIJKLM
NOPQRSTUVWX
YZabcdefghijklmn
opqrstuvwxyz123
4567890&?!ß£$(;)

HELVETICA LIGHT ITALIC

ABCDEFGHIJK
LMNOPQRST
UVWXYZabcd
efghijklmnopqr
stuvwxyz1234
567890&?!ß£$(;)

HELVETICA BOLD ITALIC

ABCDEFGHIJ
KLMNOPQRS
TUVWXYZ ab
cdefghijklmn
opqrstuvwxyz
1234567890&
?!ß£$(;)《》❊

HELVETICA EXTRA BOLD

ABCDEFGHIJK
LMNOPQRSTU
VWXYZ abcde
fghijklmnopqr
stuvwxyz1234
567890&?!ß£$
◗◖《》ñĵ

HELVETICA MEDIUM

ABCDEFGHI
JKLMNOPQ
RSTUVWXY
Z&?!ß£$《》❊

abcdefghijkl
mnopqrstuv
wxyz12345
67890;̈

HELVETICA MEDIUM

HELVETICA MEDIUM CONDENSED

ABCDEFGHIJKL
MNOPQRSTUV
WXYZabcdefgh
ijklmnopqrstuvw
xyz 123456789
0&?!ß£$(;)《》❊

HELVETICA MEDIUM EXTENDED

ABCDEFGHIJ
KLMNOPQRS
TUVWXYZ ab
cdefghijklmno
pqrstuvwxyz
1234567890&?
!ß£$(;)《》❊

HELVETICA MEDIUM ITALIC

ABCDEFGHIJK
MNOPQRSTUV
WXYZabcdefgh
ijklmnopqrstuv
wxyz 12345678
90&?!ß£$(;)《》❊

51

underscoring a word or phrase to a box or border, or horizontal or vertical column division.

Leading. The term (pronounced "ledding") comes from the days of hot-metal type, when metal strips called leads were inserted between each line of metal type, adding extra space between lines. What you are now reading was set 10 on 12. That means that the type is 10 points high with 2 points of space between lines. This was done for better readability. If a great deal of copy is set solid (no additional space between lines), it may be difficult to read. Whenever space permits, leading helps clarity.

Ems. A unit for measuring spacing such as indented paragraph openings. The em quad is a space as wide as the height of the type. An en quad is only half as wide as an em quad. The paragraph openings in this text are indented one em, or 10 points, from the left margin.

Body and display. What you are now reading is referred to as body type. Larger type used for headlines or decoratively to attract attention is known as display type.

Letter and word spacing. Just as you can control the space between lines, so can you decide on space between words and letters. How well you do this will come with experience. There are no rules, just good judgment

These four blocks of copy illustrate the use of leading or space between lines. There are no set rules or formulas for leading. Some of the factors to consider would be the typeface itself, whether it is to be set large or small, the amount of copy involved and the area you must work within. One or two points of leading usually makes for good readability. The alphabet shown at the far right is a font of 36 point display or headline type.

SOLID

The first step in the actual printing process is that of providing an assemblage of alphabetic type characters, in the style and size desired, in a form susceptible of reproduction in plate format capable of acting as the transferring medium of multiple impressions to paper or other materials. Prior to the development of mechanical composing machines, all type was set or composed by hand. To facilitate this step a series of type cases, which are wooden trays divided into compartments of varying sizes to accommodate the different letters of the alphabet, are provided. The compositor places the type in a metal tool called a composing stick.

ONE POINT LEADED

The first step in the actual printing process is that of providing an assemblage of alphabetic type characters, in the style and size desired, in a form susceptible of reproduction in plate format capable of acting as the transferring medium of multiple impressions to paper or other materials. Prior to the development of mechanical composing machines, all type was set or composed by hand. To facilitate this step a series of type cases, which are wooden trays divided into compartments of varying sizes to accommodate the different letters of the alphabet, are provided. The compositor places the

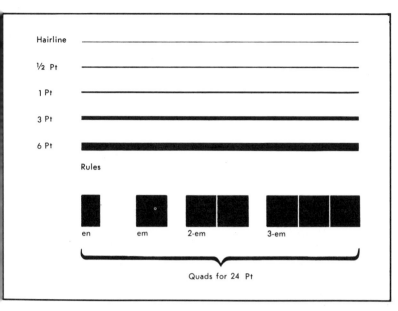

Hairline

½ Pt

1 Pt

3 Pt

6 Pt

Rules

en em 2-em 3-em

Quads for 24 Pt

TWO POINT LEADED

The first step in the actual printing process is that of providing an assemblage of alphabetic type characters, in the style and size desired, in a form susceptible of reproduction in plate format capable of acting as the transferring medium of multiple impressions to paper or other materials. Prior to the development of mechanical composing machines, **all type was set or composed by hand. To facilitate this step a series of type cases, which are wooden trays divided into compartments of varying sizes to accommodate the different letters of the alpha-**

THREE POINT LEADED

The first step in the actual printing process is that of providing an assemblage of alphabetic type characters, in the style and size desired, in a form susceptible of reproduction in plate format capable of acting as the transferring medium of multiple impressions to paper or other materials. Prior to the development of mechanical composing machines, **all type was set or composed by hand. To facilitate this step a series of type cases, which are wooden trays divided into compartments of varying sizes to**

36 point

ABCDEFGHIJKLMNOPQRSTL
UVWXYZ
rstuvwxyz
?[]†*$
abcdefghijklmnopq
1234567890
.,-:;''""!()
ABCDEFGHIJKLMNO
ABCDEFGHIJKLMNO
&

Kerning. In large type sizes, such as headlines, the apparent space between certain letters (L and T, A and W or V) is very pronounced. With handset type, the body of the type (the metal blocks on which the letters sit) must be notched—kerned—so they actually overlap slightly yet present the appearance of normal spacing. With phototype, letterspacing and kerning is easily accomplished by the keyboard operator.

Galley. Originally, the galley was a long tray in which lines of metal type were held before they were divided into separate pages. An inked impression of this standing type, a *galley proof*, was used for proofreading. Later, the corrected type would be locked up into cases for letterpress printing; or a proof of reproduction quality would be made on clay-coated paper for paste-up for an offset-printed job. With photocomposition, however, the output from the phototypesetter—in the form of long galleys of type—is of repro quality but must still be proofread. Depending on the number of corrections, corrected lines might be set as "patches" to the first galley; or the entire galley might be rerun. Because the manuscript is already on a file in the typesetters' computer memory, generating a full, revised galley takes little time.

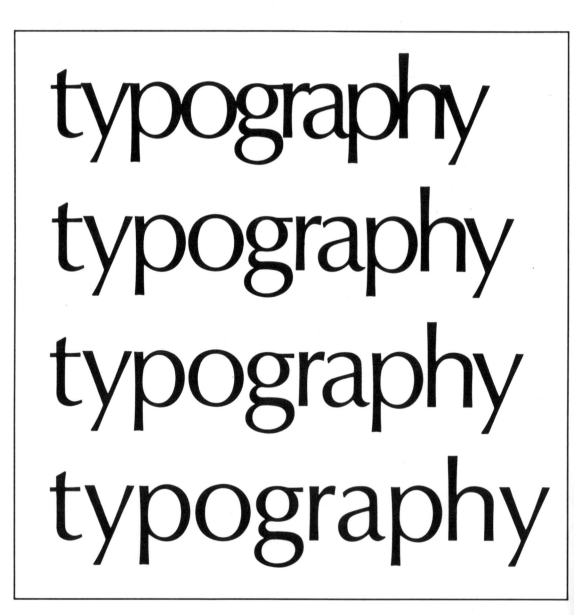

Proofreader's marks. Changes or corrections made on galley or rough proofs are usually done by using standard proofreader's marks. Some of the more commonly used ones are shown here. However, don't let these frustrate you. If any changes can be stated clearly in your own manner, a good typographer will have no trouble handling your revisions. If these marks work for you, use them—if they don't, do it your way.

Not only can you decide on space between lines, you can also determine the amount of space you may wish to use between words and even letters. As you can see in the example at left, the characters have been set in a way that ranges from tight (so that they actually overlap each other), to close, to a normal setting where neither overlapping nor touching occurs. This process of changing the letter spacing is called kerning. Once again, there are no hard-and-fast rules for doing this. Time, experience and good judgment are your best guidelines.

PROOFREADER'S MARKS

Correction Required		How to Indicate Correction
Remove letter and close up	ℰ	He marked the proof.
Remove word	ℐ	He marked the proof.
Insert space	#	He marked the proof.
Turn inverted letter	𝓰	He marked the proof.
Set in lower case	LC	He Marked the proof.
Reset in italics	ITAL.	He marked the proof.
Reset in roman (not italics)	ROM.	He marked the proof.
Reset in boldface	BF	He marked the proof.
Insert period	⊙	He marked the proof.
Transpose letters or words	TR	He (the proof marked)
Let stand as is	STET	He marked the proof.
Insert hyphen	/=/	He made the proofmark.
Equalize spacing	EQ#	He marked the proof.
Wrong font	WF	He marked the proof.
Broken letter	X	He marked the proof.
Move left (or right) to point indicated	⊏ (⊐)	⊏He marked the proof.
Insert comma	⋀	Yes he marked the proof.
Insert apostrophe	∀	He marked the boys proof.
Enclose in quotation marks	⟪ ⟫	He marked it proof.
Replace with a capital	CAP	he marked the proof.
Use small capitals	SC	He marked the proof.
Draw the word together	⌣	He m arked the proof.
Spell out word marked	SP	He marked the 2nd proof.
Add word left out	the/	He marked proof.
Start new paragraph	¶	reading. The reader marked
Run in		the proof.
Query to author	was?	The proof read by
Out of alignment. Straighten	=	He marked the proof.
Indent 1 em	☐	He marked the proof.

Fitting Copy to Your Layout

Copy, as you receive it, should be neatly typed and double-spaced on one side only of an 8½x11 sheet. Don't settle for anything less! Handwritten material, no matter how legible, should not be accepted. Anyone who tries to pass off copy to you that has been scribbled down on a pad or the back of a greasy lunch menu (and this, unfortunately, is often the case) should be warned that they're asking for trouble. An unclear beginning like this results in corrections, changes and revisions that become time-consuming and expensive.

When this happens, meeting the deadline and working with the budget becomes a frustrating experience. Try to avoid this situation by educating these amateurs as to its perils and pitfalls. You're working at being a pro —it's not unreasonable to ask others you work with to do the same.

There are several ways of transposing copy to type and making it fit your design. There is no mystery about it. It involves some simple math that can be simply solved. Here is one way to get started. As time goes on, you will, no doubt, develop your own workable method.

One thing you will need for fitting copy is a type gauge such as the one illustrated. They are inexpensive and can be purchased at any art supply store. Some type houses even give them away as promotional items. It's a good investment and should last a lifetime.

Whatever way you go about doing this, you will start by counting characters. Earlier we defined a character as an individual letter, figure or punctuation mark, or a space between words or punctuation marks. Characters are the only thing you count here—nothing but characters.

Let's use the original copy, or manuscript, from the text you are now reading as a demonstration. As I stated earlier, this book is set in the Helvetica typeface throughout. The body copy (which you are now looking at) has been set in 10 point Helvetica Lite with 2 points of leading between the lines. It has been set in a flush left, ragged right format with the longest line being 14 picas in width. To determine the space this will occupy when transposed from original copy to type, we do the following:

- On the typewritten copy, draw a light pencil line down the right side indicating the average length lines. (This is determined by eye rather than precise measurement.)
- Count the number of characters in any one line up to your pencil line.
- Count the number of lines on the page.
- Multiply the characters per line by the number of lines on the page.
- Count and add the leftover characters (the ones on the right of

HABERULE "10" TYPE GAUGE

POINT SIZE

AGATE 6 7 8 9 10 11 12

Type Size

12 point edge is also a pica rule

your pencil line), add this to your total, and you have a reasonably accurate count of the number of characters on that page.

● Referring to a type book under the Helvetica Lite listing tells us that the 10 point typeface we have chosen has about 35 characters in a line that is 14 picas in width. By dividing this number into the total character count on the page of your original copy, the result will indicate how many lines deep (how long a column) your copy will be when set in type. Using your type gauge, find the appropriate slot next to the type size you have chosen. Read down to the final figure you calculated, and

this will show you how deep your copy will appear. Remember to include the leading between lines. If we are working with 10 point type and 2 points of leading, use the 12 point measure. (Note that this 12 point edge is also used as a pica rule, since 12 points equal 1 pica.)

Once you start working with type, you will acquire a type book easily. In fact, you'll probably acquire several. The type houses want your business

and will provide you with the information you need to use their services. Most books have a table that shows the number of characters in various pica widths for any chosen typeface. If it doesn't, all you need do is to mark off the desired pica width on the example in the book and count those characters. (Be sure to count the spaces between words and punctuation marks.) The result should be the same as shown in the scale.

```
14   HELV. B.      ┌─ ( Fitting Copy to your Layout
6°   U/LC.

BODY ~
10  HELV. LITE U/LC.
12   F/C R/R
X 14 PX MAX.
2½ PTS. W/S
```

Fitting Copy to your Layout

Copy, as you receive it, should be neatly typed and double spaced on one side only of an 8 1/2 x 11 sheet. Don't settle for anything less! Handwritten material, no matter how legible, and it usually isn't, should not be accepted. Anyone who tries to pass off copy to you that has been scribbled down on a pad or the back of a greasy lunch menu, and this unfortunatly, is often the case, should be warned that they're asking for trouble. An unclear beginning like this results in corrections, changes and revisions that become time consuming and expensive.

When this happens, meeting the deadline and working within the budget becomes a frustrating experience. Try to avoid this situation by educating these ametuers as to its perils and pitfalls. You're working at being a pro... it's not unreasonable to ask others you work with to do the same.

There are several ways of transposing copy to type and making it fit your design. There is no big complicated mystery about it. It involves some simple math, and as I confessed earlier to not being a whiz at mathematics, I once again intend to present this as simply and directly as possible. What I offer here is a starting point. As time goes on your curiousity for experimentation will eventually result in your own way of doing this, which is the way it should be.

One thing you will need for this business of fitting copy is a type gauge (like the one illustrated.) They are inexpensive and can be purchased in any art supply store. Some type houses even give them away as a promotional item. It's a good investment and will last a lifetime, unless you use it to swat flies.

This is a page of typewritten manuscript that has been "marked up" for type. The notations in the left margin tell the typographer what typeface is to be used, its size, how wide it is to be set and how much leading and wordspacing will be needed. The end result of this is the body copy you just read on the opposite page.

Small Space Ads Using Type Only

Here is a series of newspaper ads for the Westport Broadcasting Company. As you can see, they employ no illustration at all, just type. They were designed to be used in several local newspapers, each of which had their own definition of just how wide a column should be. With the exception of the call letters WMMM, which is a display face called Avant Garde, all the other copy was set in Helvetica. Another consideration was given to the generous use of white space or "air" around the type. Although they may have somewhat of a stark look as you see them here, bear in mind that each one had to stand alone on a newspaper page where it had to compete with all the other ads and editorial matter that was presented on that page. The use of white space or air helped to set them apart and created the *visual hook* needed to draw the viewers' interest and overcome the handicap of the ads' relatively small size.

I was told by the station's general manager that everyone concerned was pleased with how the ads looked and impressed with the response that resulted from their use.

And that's what it's all about.

We're the one to turn to... for the very best in Music, News, Weather, Sports, and more...more of everything for everyone in Fairfield County

We're the one to turn to

WMMM

1260AM on your dial

**We're the
one to turn to...**
for the very best
in Music, News,
Weather, Sports,
and more...more of
everything
for everyone
in Fairfield
County

We're the one to turn to
WMMM
1260 AM on your dial

We're the one to turn to...
for the very best in
Music, News, Weather, Sports and more...
more of everything for everyone
in Fairfield County

We're the one to turn to
WMMM
1260 AM on your dial

When Only a Word or Two Is Needed

Sometimes a job calls for only one or two words or possibly a short line. To order this from a typographer might not be economical. An economical answer could be found in using dry transfer lettering, available at any art supply store. Depending on the manufacturer, they vary in cost and application, but the results are similar. The example here shows what can be achieved when your design requires a limited number of words.

This is one of those think-big-but-cheap jobs I mentioned earlier. I received a call from a local shop that sells custom imprinted sportswear. They had been contracted to design and print the team shirts for a ladies running club called the "Jogging Jills." As printers, and not designers, they asked if I could develop a design within the framework of their "limited budget." I accepted the challenge.

In order to keep costs down, I used some dry transfer lettering from my files. Once the words were spelled out or "set," I enlarged them to the sizes I needed by the use of photostats. (We will discuss photostats in detail in Section 3.) Type alone didn't seem to be enough to convey the desired feeling for "Jogging Jills." By using the letter "O" in the word "jog" as a

background and refreshing my mind with a book on anatomy, I was able to work in a pair of stylized running female legs. This seemed to make the design work. The final art was eventually silk screened (a printing process we will also discuss in Section 3) onto the tee shirts and running jackets. Everyone was happy — the printers, the ladies and I. All's well that ends well, but it wasn't quite over. A few weeks later I had another call from the sportswear shop requesting another design. Apparently the ladies' husbands had formed their own running club and were calling themselves the "Jogging Jocks." What I did for them appears on page 15.

Putting it All Together

Preparing Your Design for Reproduction

You have now reached the point where you are ready to put your design into final form for the printer. What you are about to make is something called a mechanical, keyline or a paste-up. Call it what you will, it amounts to the same thing—all of your design elements in their exact position on a piece of mounting or illustration board. Once completed and approved, this becomes "camera ready" copy. That means the printer can now photograph your work, and with the resulting negatives make the necessary plates which will transform what you have carefully assembled into the desired number of printed sheets. How well you've done your job will now be decided by the public for whom the message was intended.

The Printing Process

The three most commonly used printing processes are offset, letterpress and silk screen. The details of these procedures can be most complex; however, the principles involved are rather simple to understand. As a graphic designer, you should understand these principles and have a good working knowledge of reproduction methods. That is, you should have a good idea of what happens when your work goes to press. Beyond that, the real interest is in seeing the final result.

Some graphic designers become fascinated by printing and all its ramifications. This is understandable, as they are engrossing procedures. However, there is no need for you to become a production expert. With this in mind, let's approach the subject as simply as possible to give you a working knowledge as a guide for

preparing designs for reproduction. If you feel the need for further information, there are many technical books available. Also recommended is a guided tour through a printing plant to give you a firsthand look at how things are done. Printers, like good artists, are proud of what they do. You should have little difficulty in arranging an invitation to see what goes on at the plant that prints your work.

Offset

Of all the printing processes being used today, the offset method is far and away the most common; its economy and flexibility is virtually unmatched by anything else. Probably about 90 percent of all the printed material you see has been reproduced by an offset method.

Essentially, printing by offset begins with the wrapping of a printing plate around a cylinder. It is then inked. The inked image is transferred (offset) to another cylinder carrying a rubber *blanket* which rolls against the plate.

The image is then transferred to paper over which the blanket passes. Although greatly simplified, this is basically all there is to the offset method.

Full-color offset printing is a particularly complex procedure, but today it is accomplished with great skill and accuracy in every part of the

world. Improved presses, computer controls, and laser beam scanning have done much to advance the quality and effectiveness of color reproduction.

Full-color printing is usually limited to three colors—red, yellow, and blue, plus black. A plate is made for each color, and one for the black. When they are printed one over another, the result is a fairly accurate representation of a full range of color. If you examine a printed color piece with a power lens or magnifying glass, you would see dots of each color and black positioned next to one another in such a way that, to the naked eye, they create the illusion of multiple mixed hues.

This is virtually the same principle employed by the artists of the Pointillist school of painting. This procedure, sometimes called *Divisionism*, is accomplished by painting tiny spots of pure color next to each other throughout the picture. For example, dots of red and yellow used side by side blend optically to create the visual impression of orange. The effects are quite remarkable both in painting and in printing.

Letterpress

If you've ever used a rubber stamp and ink pad, then you've employed the principle of the letterpress process. Printing by letterpress involves a metal

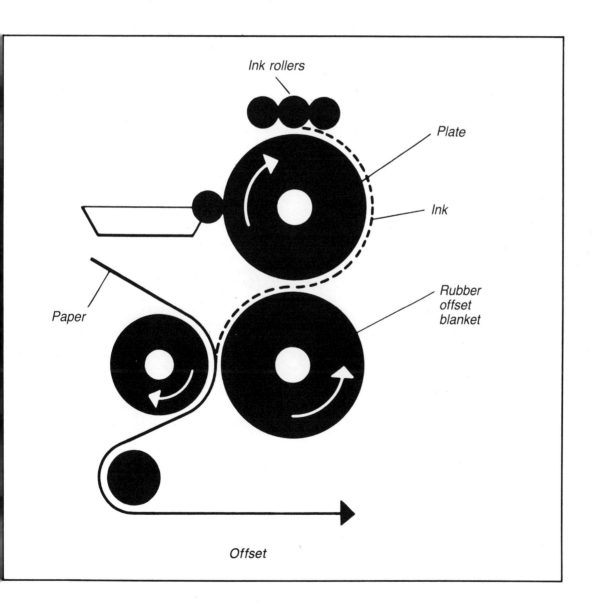

Offset

plate with a raised image that is placed on a press, inked by rollers, and pressed against the surface to be printed, usually paper.

Although this procedure sounds simpler than offset, the "make-ready" time, that is, the time it takes to prepare the press and make a printing plate from final art, is more time-consuming and expensive than offset. The letterpress process still enjoys limited use, but its output is small compared to offset.

Silk Screen

This process is widely used for printing on surfaces other than paper. The dashboard of your car is a good example. The numbers and calibrations on the instruments as well as the identifications of knobs and switches were most likely put on there by silk-screen printing. Round or curved surfaces are also ideally suited for this process. The creation of plastic has spawned new innovations in package design. Virtually all graphics for plastic containers of any conceivable size or shape are printed by silk screen. Face panels on stereos radios and cassette recorders are other examples—the list goes on.

No matter where you live, there's likely to be a printer nearby. In particular, quick copy centers have spread almost everywhere in recent

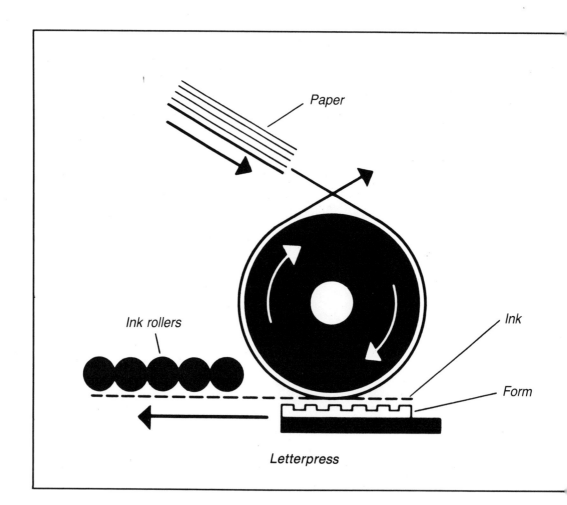

Letterpress

years. Their services run from the simple duplicating of typewritten pages to short-run offset printing of varying quality and cost. The larger printing houses are also in abundance, and competition among them is fierce, giving you the advantage of demanding high quality at a competitive cost.

Sooner or later you will get to know them, and they will come to know you, and it is in their environs your education in printing methods will come into focus. What you need to concern yourself with here is the preparation of your design for reproduction no matter which process is used.

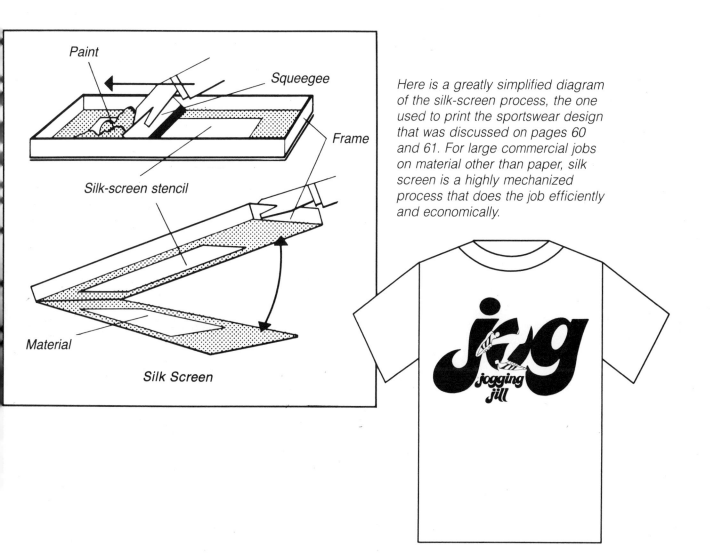

Paint

Squeegee

Frame

Silk-screen stencil

Material

Silk Screen

Here is a greatly simplified diagram of the silk-screen process, the one used to print the sportswear design that was discussed on pages 60 and 61. For large commercial jobs on material other than paper, silk screen is a highly mechanized process that does the job efficiently and economically.

Making a Mechanical

Organization is the key word here. When I think of organization, this is the definition I have in mind: "First, plan your work—and then work your plan."

The making of a mechanical, as you will soon discover, involves putting together many bits and pieces. Often you will be working under the pressure of a deadline. Getting organized at the beginning and staying organized is your best assurance that the job will move along smoothly, because you stay in control.

A mechanical is a working drawing or guide for the printer showing all of your design elements in their exact position. This is done on a sheet of lightweight illustration or mounting board. Even though the final printed piece may be in color, the mechanical is executed in black and white. Any element that prints in color is indicated on a tissue overlay along with any other explanations or instructions to the printer. All the elements employed to make a mechanical must be "line copy." Any black-and-white tonal art such as a painting or photograph must be converted to line copy by having them made into a "halftone." A full color photo is indicated by a black-and-white print such as a photostat or other facsimile to show its size and

osition. The art itself accompanies
the mechanical separately with
necessary instructions.

Line Art

Any drawing or graphic symbol that
has been rendered in solid black on a
white surface qualifies as line copy.
Type is also line copy. Even though
many of these elements may eventually
be printed in color, they must start out
as black-and-white line copy on the
mechanical.

*These are all examples of line art.
Whether it be illustration or type, if it
has been rendered in solid black on a
white surface it is line art. Although
they may eventually print in color or
even on colored paper, on the
mechanical they must be in black and
white.*

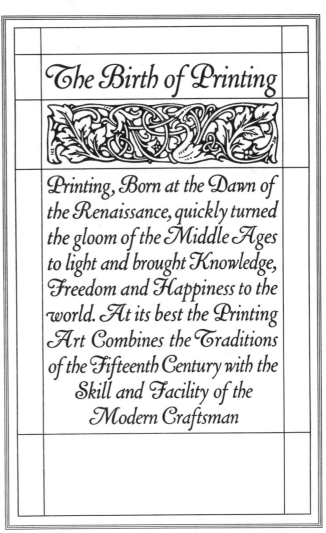

Halftone Art

A painting or photograph, known as continuous-tone art, must be converted to line copy before it can be printed. This is done photo-mechanically by a printer or engraver. The engraver photographs the original art through a halftone screen which transforms the image on film into a series of dots.

A halftone in a newspaper is a good example. You can easily see the dot pattern with the naked eye, because the halftone was made with a "65-line-screen." This term means that the screen used produces 65 dots to the inch. Halftone screens are available in a wide range, from 55, 65, 85, 100, 110, 133, 150, 175—all the way up to 300 dots per inch.

The size of the screen to be used for any given job is determined by the paper to be printed on. Pulp paper, such as newsprint, requires a coarse screen such as a 65-line for best reproduction. Conversely, the glossy, "slick" paper used in the better quality magazines can handle a screen range of 133, 150 or even higher. Most magazine reproductions use a 133-line screen which produces over 17,000 dots per square inch. The higher you go with your screen number, the more difficult it is to tell a halftone from a continuous tone.

Here's what happens when you take a piece of continuous-tone art such as a painting or a photograph and "shoot" or photograph it as line art. Depending on the subject matter, the result can sometimes be interesting from a design point of view, but for a more accurate reproduction a halftone screen must be used.

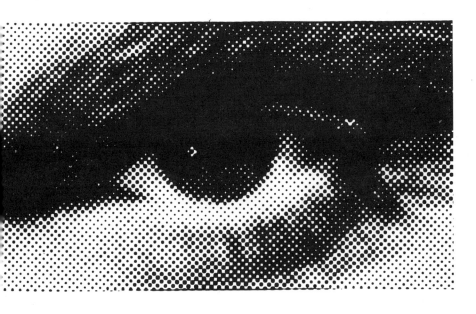

Here's the same photograph shot using a 65-line halftone screen. It is now ready for reproduction, because it had been converted to line art. Sixty-five-line is a fairly coarse screen that enables you to see the screen or dot pattern with the naked eye. Above is a greatly magnified section of the right eye that leaves no doubt as to the screen pattern. The tonal effect of the photo is maintained by the varying sizes of the dots—light areas have smaller dots and hold less ink than dark areas.

Photostats

A photostat, or *stat* as it's commonly called, is a sharp photographic print made from a piece of original line art. They are most helpful when it comes to making a mechanical. There was a time when they were not considered to be either accurate or reliable, but computerized technology and improved processing methods have raised their quality from a cheap and quick photoprint to an excellent, reproducible line copy.

Not only can a stat faithfully duplicate your original, it can enlarge, reduce or even reverse it. Reversing is the process of making what is black, white, and what is white, black. This is called a *negative* and makes possible many different design approaches. Most well-equipped art departments have their own stat machines, and with a minimum of instruction you can operate them inside of an hour, no matter how complicated they may look. If one is not available, most printers and quick copy centers have photostat services available at reasonable cost.

Aa Aa
AaAa

Enlarging, Reducing, and Cropping

It's a rare situation when the illustrations you are working with are the size you need for the job at hand. They usually have to be enlarged or reduced. When using a photograph, it is likely to need cropping before it can be sized.

Scaling a picture up or down (so it can be reproduced larger or smaller) is a simple procedure. As the diagram shows, if you run a diagonal line from the lower left corner through the upper right corner, you can enlarge or reduce both height and width proportionately. This should be done with a soft pencil on a sheet of tracing paper over the art. In scaling a silhouette, frame it first with a line around all four sides and then follow the same procedure.

Cropping a picture requires, above all else, common sense and good judgment. There's more to it than just making it fit your layout. Try to get the most out of a picture by eliminating all nonessentials and playing up its story aspects.

There are several commercial cropping devices available, but I think most of them are a waste of time and money. The easily made pieces of L-shaped cardboard croppers shown here do the job with speed and accuracy.

Once your cropping has been decided, take a grease pencil, and holding your frames in place, draw your cropped outline directly on the photograph. The grease pencil is soft and won't hurt the surface, and it can be rubbed off later. (This applies only to glossy photos. Never mark directly on photos printed on dull-finish or uncoated papers.) The photograph can now be scaled for size using the cropped outline as your guide.

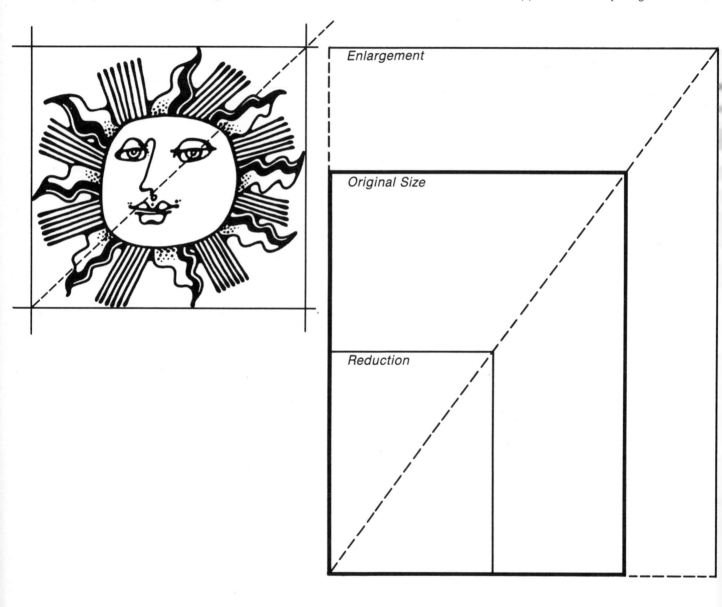

Enlargement

Original Size

Reduction

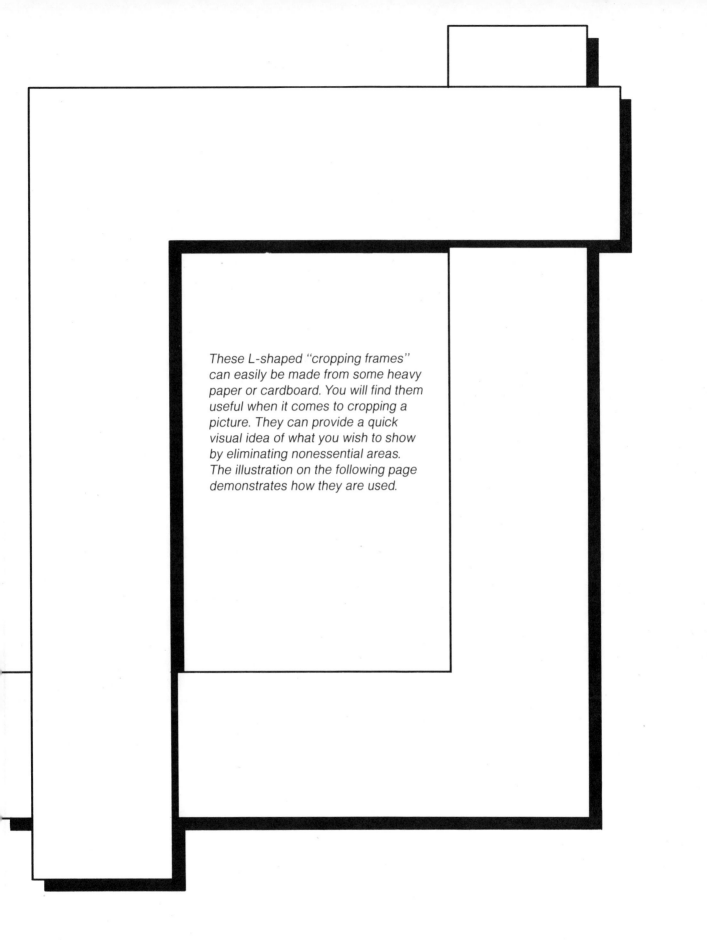

These L-shaped "cropping frames" can easily be made from some heavy paper or cardboard. You will find them useful when it comes to cropping a picture. They can provide a quick visual idea of what you wish to show by eliminating nonessential areas. The illustration on the following page demonstrates how they are used.

Place the frames over the picture until you're satisfied with the way it looks. Hold the frames firmly in place and with a grease pencil draw your cropped outline directly on the photograph. Using this outline as a guide, you can now scale your picture up or down in size as desired.

Computing Sizes

Don't let what you see here upset you. Realize what we've been getting into — getting more technical as we go, but it is all still pretty simple if taken slowly, one step at a time.

Shown here is a proportional scale, used to size art and photos for the printer. Such *sizing* is usually indicated as a percentage of the original, because the cameras used for these operations are calibrated in percents, not inches.

Here's an example: If you have a piece of art that is 10 inches high and you want to reduce it to 5 inches in height, then it would be half the size or 50 percent. That's easy. You can figure it out in your head. But, if that same piece of art which is 10 inches high is to be reduced to, let's say, 7⅜ inches high . . . trying to figure that one out could give you a headache. The "wheel," as it is commonly called, will give you the answer quickly and accurately. Find the size of your original art, in this case 10 inches, on the inside wheel and line it up with the size you want, 7⅜ inches, on the outside wheel. Then look in the window where it says "percentage of original size" and you'll find that the answer is 74 percent. Simple.

This inexpensive tool can be found in any art supply store, but I've never heard of anyone buying one. They're readily available in any art department, and most printers or stat houses give them away as promotional items.

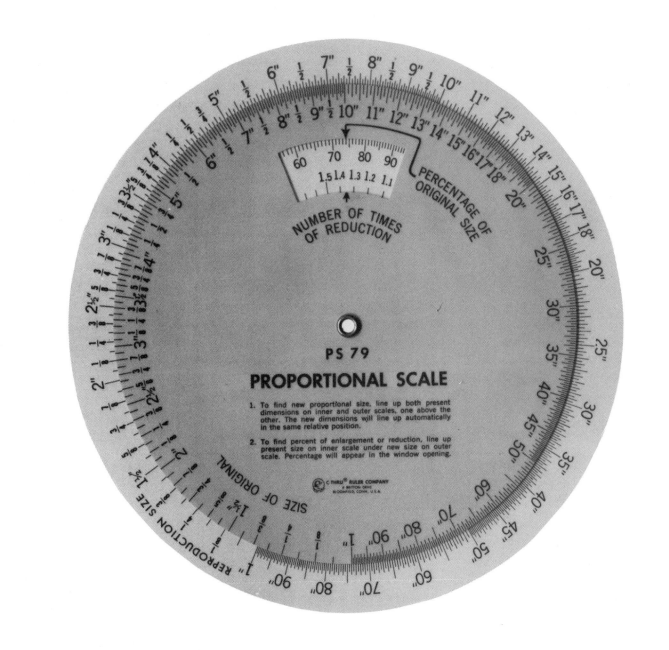

Tools and Materials

Here is another area where it is best to stress simplicity. Every time I walk into a well-stocked art supply store I have mixed feelings of amazement and confusion by what is offered. I've put together more camera ready art than I'd care to admit to, and I've always done it with the same simple tools and materials that I am about to outline here.

All the so-called timesaving gadgets that guarantee to raise the quality of your work to new heights of perfection rest in a fringe area that has little effect on your effort or result. They're gadgets, and the people who get lured into buying and using them are gadgeteers. Professional quality finished art does not depend on gadgets. It's achieved with a few simple tools and materials.

Although the end result may be the same, no two designers make a mechanical the exact same way. You too will soon develop your own approach, and with that in mind, the following list is a basic one that you may wish to change, add to or subtract from. Suit yourself, but whatever you decide, be in control.

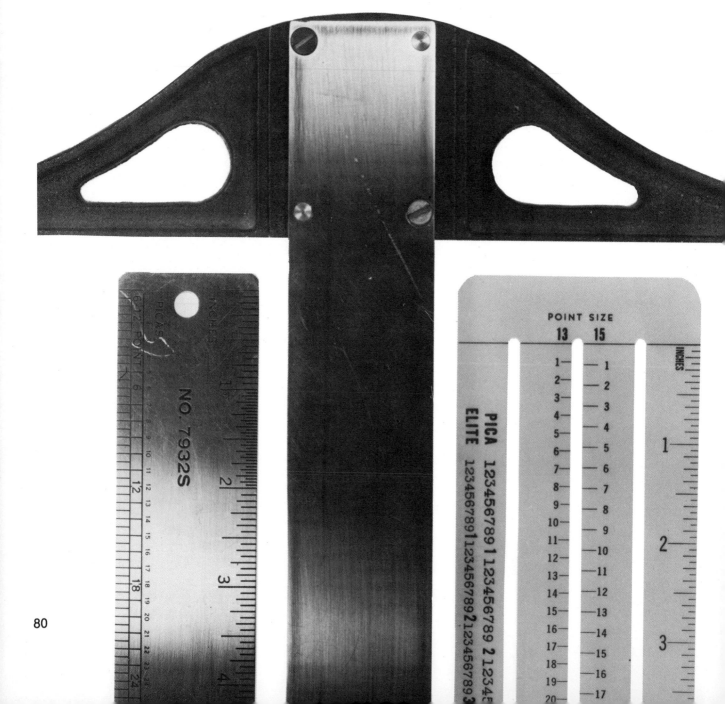

Don't let any tool or material dictate how you do the job at hand.

- A T-square, ruler and at least one triangle will be needed for drawing or ruling accurate horizontal and vertical lines.
- Masking tape—Needed to firmly secure your working surface to the drawing board.
  Blue pencil—A light blue pencil should be used when laying out dimensions and guide lines. When your mechanical is photographed to make a printing plate, these blue lines will not reproduce.
  Ink, brush, opaque white—A bottle of waterproof black India ink and at least one good sable watercolor

brush. No. 2 is a useful size. Opaque white watercolor is used to clean up any small errors that can happen when inking.

● Ruling pen, compass, dividers—It's not necessary to buy a complete set of drawing instruments. (I own a set, and the only pieces I ever use are the ruling pen, compass and dividers. The rest of it is on a shelf collecting dust.) A ruling pen and compass will be necessary to render lines and circles in ink. If you've never used these tools before, they may seem awkward at first, but so was learning to drive a car. A little practice and they will soon become second nature to

you. There are mechanical pens such as Rapidograph, Refograph and others that will also do the job. Experiment if you like and see which suits your working methods best. You will find a pair of dividers useful when dividing a line or circle into equal parts as well as transferring measurements from one spot to another.

● Razor blades, scissors—To be used, naturally, for cutting and trimming. Some designers prefer an X-acto knife to a razor blade, but whatever you decide on, these are necessary tools to cut and trim your elements before positioning them on your mechanical.

● Tweezers—A small but very useful tool. You will find yourself using this constantly for handling your freshly cemented pieces, especially the smaller ones.

● Rubber cement—A universally used adhesive for making mechanicals. It is inexpensive and easy to use. For overall versatility, rubber cement is hard to beat. When using rubber cement if you go beyond the desired area, you just let it dry and it rubs off easily with a *pick-up*—an eraser-like piece of hardened rubber cement that can be purchased in art supply stores. The cement can be removed from almost any surface without leaving a mark. Elements that have been mounted can be adjusted or removed by applying a little rubber-cement thinner, letting it seep under the edges to temporarily loosen the cement. The thinner is usually stored in a dispenser that looks like a small oil can. This allows you to apply the thinner along the edges of an element, and as it seeps in, you can easily lift it up and off. A small eye-dropper bottle can also be used for this purpose. *Rubber cement and thinner are highly flammable. Use them safely by keeping them capped and away from heat or an open flame.*

- Wax—Applied with a hand applicator or a desktop machine, this wax remains tacky indefinitely.

Unlike rubber cement, waxed copy need not be put in position immediately. In fact, it will still be ready to use weeks later. Waxed art and type may be shifted around on the mechanical board until the most satisfactory position is determined. The waxed items must then be burnished thoroughly—rubbed with a hard, smooth tool which adheres them to the mechanical board. (To avoid possible damage to type or art, you may place a sheet of tracing paper over it and rub on that.) Waxed copy is easy to put in position, easy to pick up and reposition, and won't leave you with sticky fingers.

The end result.

The Mechanical

The best way to show how a mechanical is made is to make one. So the next few pages will be devoted to doing exactly that. This step-by-step demonstration will outline the preparation of a simple mechanical involving type (line art) and a photograph (continuous-tone art which must be converted to halftone), and which will finally print in one color, black. The following procedure holds true for any mechanical, no matter how many elements may be involved. They are no more difficult to do; they just take longer. Now, let's organize our tools, materials, and most important, our thinking, and get going.

Preliminary Layout

Most mechanical work is done on a smooth surfaced illustration board. There are several brands available—take your choice. For this demonstration, I am using Bainbridge number 172. I also keep a spare piece on hand to use as a cutting and pasting board.

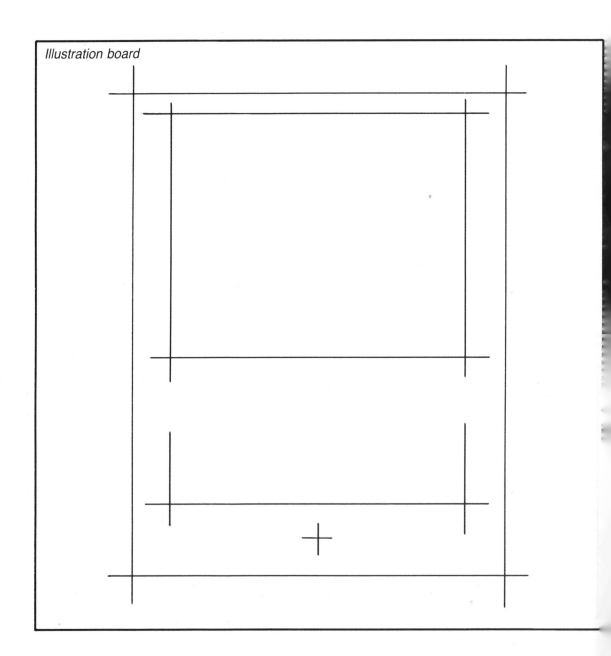

Illustration board

Begin by squaring up your working surface on your drawing board and securing it firmly with masking tape. Now, using your T-square, triangle and light blue pencil, indicate the outside dimensions of the printing area. The illustration board should be large enough to allow at least 2 inches of margin all around. Most mechanicals are done the same size as the final printed piece, but there are exceptions. A poster, for instance, which measures 3x4 feet in size might be more conveniently done on the drawing board if it were executed at half its size, or 18x24 inches. On the other hand, a postage stamp design would be easier to do if you were able to work four or five times larger than the final reproduction size.

Next, indicate the position of all elements of art and type. Don't hesitate to overdraw these areas. Light blue does not photograph in the plate-making process, so make the lines long enough so that they are not covered up when pasting down the art.

Printer's Marks

The next step involves the indication of reference marks for the printer. They are cropmarks, folding lines and holding lines, and they must be drawn with either a red or black pen so that they will show when a negative is made prior to making a plate.

Although light blue doesn't photograph, red does, the same as black, so when you want something to show, use red or black.

Cropmarks, drawn as shown at all four corners, indicate the outside dimensions of the job. They also tell the printer where the final printed piece is to be trimmed so it will be the correct size. If a printed piece is to be folded, a broken line is drawn outside the trim area to show exactly where. A holding line shows the exact area that will be occupied by a halftone or piece or art that will accompany the mechanical with instructions for the printer to strip into that area when making his negative.

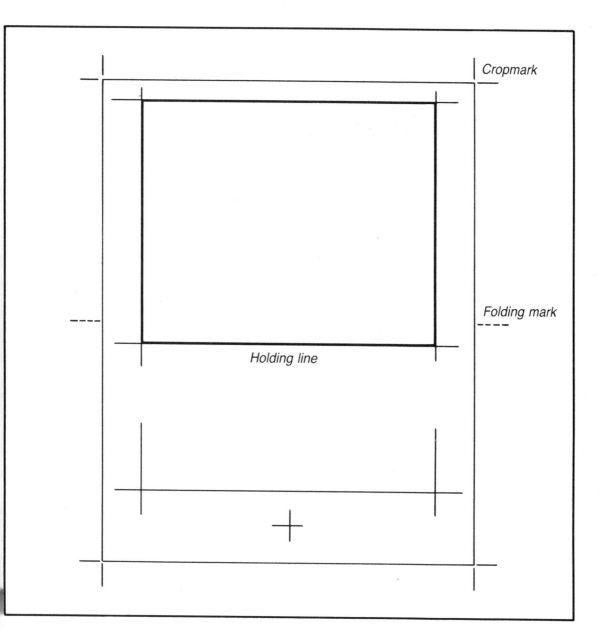

Cropmark

Folding mark

Holding line

Handling the Halftone

The making of a mechanical is either done by working from the top down, or by putting down the largest or key element first, and then relating all else to it. In this case, we're doing both. The halftone is the largest of the three elements, and it's at the top of the design. There are several ways to show the size and position of a halftone on a mechanical.

The first, as was stated earlier, is to draw a holding line, either red or black, that shows the exact area the halftone will occupy.

The second is to make a stat or even a Xerox copy of the photograph and paste it into the exact position where you want the halftone to appear. They may be poor copies of the photograph, but they will be good enough to show the printer where the halftone will go.

The third way is to use a piece of red self-adhesive acetate. Cut it slightly larger than the halftone area. Lay it down, and then with your T-square, triangle and razor blade, trim it to size. By using red acetate, you

will be able to see the holding line so you can make an accurate cut. As far as the camera is concerned, it's black. When a negative is made it becomes a clear area or "window" where the halftone will be stripped in.

In all three cases, the printer makes the line negative of the type and the halftone negative in separate processes, "stripping" (taping) them together before making the printing plate.

The fourth method, and the one we are using here, involves the use of a "velox." A velox is a screened photoprint of continuous-tone copy that can be put directly on the mechanical. Because the velox is line

copy, the printer can shoot a negative of the whole mechanical in one step. Assuming that this job is to be reproduced in a newspaper, this velox was made with a 65-line screen.

To position the velox on the mechanical, first tape it to your cutting board, and then, with your T-square, triangle and razor blade, trim it to size.

Next turn it face down and give the back a coat of rubber cement. While that's drying, coat the area on your illustration board where it will be positioned. Don't worry about overdoing it. Once the velox is down and set, all excess cement can be easily cleaned off with your pick-up. When both surfaces are dry, a slip

sheet (tracing paper is good) is placed on the board, and the velox is placed over the slip sheet. Line up the velox at the top edge of the holding line. When you're satisfied as to its position, slowly remove the slip sheet. Then take a clean sheet of tracing paper, lay it over the velox, and press it firmly down. This method is called "dry cement mounting" and works well for handling large pieces of copy.

Red or black holding line.

Stat or photocopy.

Red self-adhesive film or acetate.

65 line screen velox.

Type and Signature

These two elements are not large, and they can be put into place by coating the backside of each and letting them dry. When you're ready to position the copy "movies," coat the area on the board with cement and place the copy down immediately. This will give you about 15 or 20 seconds to slide it into position and get it properly aligned with your T-square. Do the same with the other element, and then again using your tracing paper, press them down firmly. Once dry and set, they can be cleaned off with your pick-up. This method is called . . . you guessed it, "wet cement mounting."

Let's assume that part of this job requires you to design and execute finished art for the signature or trademark. In order to do this you would take your design at top left and from it make a negative stat that you see at top right. Next, as lower left shows, you scribe a circle with an ink compass and then carefully fill it in using a sable watercolor brush and India ink. Finally, trim the negative stat and paste it in the circle. Take care the edges you trimmed on the stat have been also blackened, or they may show through as white cut marks in an area you wanted solid black.

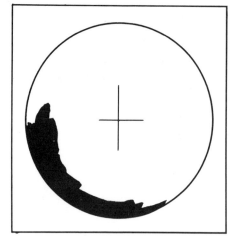

Handling Separate Art

Any piece of art or photograph that is to accompany the mechanical should be mounted on heavy board with a tissue or other paper overlay for protection. Allow enough margin on the board to accommodate any pertinent information such as cropmarks, sizes or key numbers. Key numbers or letters are used to designate any piece of art that has been indicated on the mechanical by a holding line, stat, facsimile copy, or acetate window. These areas are marked, usually with a red pen or pencil, as 1, 2, 3, or A, B, C, and corresponding numbers or letters are used on the accompanying art to show the printer exactly where everything goes.

In this whole operation, handle everything—illustrations, photographs, copy, mechanicals—with care and respect. Use common sense—don't write or mark on glossy photographs with anything but a soft grease pencil. Don't use paper clips; don't fold or roll; don't trim to size. Tell the printer to be careful and to handle all art with care. This work represents much effort on the part of artist and photographer, and although you may not be working for posterity, who knows, the material may be used again at some future time.

A Final Word

There isn't a book around, no matter how detailed or well written, that can provide the solid education that results from the daily experience of trial and error. This work is no exception. What I've tried to demonstrate are flexible guidelines rather than a rigid, one-way approach. Use these guidelines as you will; some you will find useful, others you may wish to ignore. There will come a time when you will be doing things your own way, on your own terms. This is as it should be. That's when you've become a seasoned pro. It'll happen, you'll see.

There's an old school building near where I live. Above its main entrance, handsomely chiseled in classic Roman letters, is an inscription that reads: *"Be true to your work, and your work will be true to you."* That pretty well says it for graphic design—or any other worthy endeavor. And graphic design is a worthy endeavor . . . so long as you don't just sit around waiting for that "Big Job" to come to you. It won't. Any job is only as big as the artist who does it. Always give it your best effort, and you'll never have reason to apologize or make excuses for what you've done.

If you were to go back into art history, you would find that many of the great artists of their time were also involved in graphics. Along with Toulouse-Lautrec, there were Dürer, Goya, Hogarth, Daumier, Forain, Delacroix, Cassatt, Munch, Chagall, and many more. True, most of these talents were not concerned with doing mechanicals and pasting up type, but they were deeply involved with excellence in reproduction. I'd say we're traveling in good company, and I intend to try to maintain those standards. How about you?

Index

Other Art Books from North Light

Graphics/Business of Art

Airbrush Workbooks (4 in series) $7.95 each

The Art & Craft of Greeting Cards, by Susan Evarts $15.95 (paper)

An Artist's Guide to Living By Your Brush Alone, by Edna Wagner Piersol $9.95 (paper)

Artist's Market: Where & How to Sell Your Graphic Art (Annual Directory) $18.95 (cloth)

Basic Graphic Design & Paste-Up, by Jack Warren $12.95 (paper)

Complete Airbrush & Photoretouching Manual, by Peter Owen & John Sutcliffe $23.95 (cloth)

The Complete Guide to Greeting Card Design & Illustration, by Eva Szela $24.95 (cloth)

Color Harmony: A Guide to Creative Color Combinations, by Hideaki Chijiiwa $14.95 (paper)

The Complete Guide to Framing, by Jenny Rodwell $16.95 (cloth)

Design Rendering Techniques, by Dick Powell $27.95 (cloth)

Dynamic Airbrush, by David Miller & James Effler $29.95 (cloth)

Fashion Illustration Workbooks (4 in series) $7.95 each

Getting It Printed, by Beach, Shepro & Russon $29.50 (paper)

The Graphic Arts Studio Manual, by Bert Braham $22.95 (cloth)

Marker Rendering Techniques, by Dick Powell & Patricia Monahan $32.95 (cloth)

The Graphic Artist's Guide to Marketing & Self-Promotion, by Sally Prince Davis $15.95 (paper)

Graphic Tools & Techniques, by Laing & Saunders-Davies $24.95 (cloth)

Graphics Handbook, by Howard Munce $12.95 (paper)

How to Draw & Sell Cartoons, by Ross Thomson & Bill Hewison $15.95 (cloth)

How to Draw & Sell Comic Strips, by Alan McKenzie $18.95 (cloth)

How to Understand & Use Design & Layout, by Alan Swann $22.95 (cloth)

Illustration & Drawing: Styles & Techniques, by Terry Presnall $22.95 (cloth)

The North Light Art Competition Handbook, by John M. Angelini $9.95 (paper)

North Light Dictionary of Art Terms, by Margy Lee Elspass $10.95 (paper)

Presentation Techniques for the Graphic Artist, by Jenny Mulherin $24.95 (cloth)

Print Production Handbook, by David Bann $14.95 (cloth)

Studio Secrets for the Graphic Artist, by Graham et al $27.50 (cloth)

Type: Design, Color, Character & Use, by Michael Beaumont $24.95 (cloth)

Watercolor

Basic Watercolor Painting, by Judith Campbell-Reed $15.95 (paper)

Capturing Mood in Watercolor, by Phil Austin, $21.95 (cloth)

Getting Started in Watercolor, by John Blockley $17.95 (paper)

Make Your Watercolors Sing, by LaVere Hutchings $22.95 (cloth)

Painting Flowers with Watercolor, by Ethel Todd George $17.95 (paper)

Painting in Watercolors, edited by Yvonne Deutsch $18.95 (cloth)

Painting Nature's Details in Watercolor, by Cathy Johnson $24.95 (cloth)

Transparent Watercolor, by Edward D. Walker $24.95 (cloth)

Watercolor Energies, by Frank Webb $17.95 (paper)

Watercolor for All Seasons, by Elaine and Murray Wentworth $21.95 (cloth)

Watercolor Interpretations, by John Blockley $19.95 (paper)

Watercolor Options, by Ray Loos $22.50 (cloth)

Watercolor Painting on Location, by El Meyer $19.95 (cloth)

Watercolor—The Creative Experience, by Barbara Nechis $16.95 (paper)

Watercolor Tricks & Techniques, by Cathy Johnson $24.95 (cloth)

Watercolor Workbook, by Bud Biggs & Lois Marshall $18.95 (paper)

Watercolor: You Can Do It!, by Tony Couch $24.95 (cloth)

Wet Watercolor, by Wilfred Ball $24.95 (cloth)

Watercolor Videos

Watercolor Fast & Loose, with Ron Ranson $29.95 (VHS or Beta)

Watercolor Pure & Simple, with Ron Ranson $29.95 (VHS or Beta)

Mixed Media

A Basic Course in Design, by Ray Prohaska $12.95 (paper)

The Basis of Successful Art: Concept and Composition, by Fritz Henning $16.95 (paper)

Calligraphy Workbooks (4 in series) $7.95 each

Catching Light in Your Paintings, by Charles Sovek $16.95 (paper)

Colored Pencil Drawing Techniques, by Iain Hutton-Jamieson $22.95 (cloth)

Creative Drawing & Painting, by Brian Bagnall $29.95 (cloth)

Drawing & Painting with Ink, by Fritz Henning $24.95 (cloth)

Drawing & Painting Animals, by Fritz Henning $14.95 (paper)

Drawing & Painting Buildings, by Reggie Stanton $19.95 (cloth)

Drawing By Sea & River, by John Croney $14.95 (cloth)

Drawing for Pleasure, edited by Peter D. Johnson $15.95 (paper)

Encyclopaedia of Drawing, by Clive Ashwin $22.50 (cloth)

Exploring Color, by Nita Leland $26.95 (cloth)

The Eye of the Artist, by Jack Clifton $14.95 (paper)

The Figure, edited by Walt Reed $15.95 (paper)

Flower Painting, by Jenny Rodwell $19.95 (cloth)

Keys to Drawing, by Bert Dodson $21.95 (cloth)

Landscape Painting, by Patricia Monahan $19.95 (cloth)

The North Light Handbook of Artist's Materials, by Ian Hebblewhite $24.95 (cloth)

The North Light Illustrated Book of Painting Techniques, by Elizabeth Tate $26.95 (cloth)

On Drawing and Painting, by Paul Land $15.95 (cloth)

Painting & Drawing Boats, by Moira Huntley $16.95 (paper)

Painting Birds & Animals, by Patricia Monahan $21.95 (cloth)

Painting a Likeness, by Douglas Graves $19.95 (cloth)

Painting Nature, by Franklin Jones $17.95 (paper)

Painting Portraits, by Jenny Rodwell $21.95 (cloth)

Painting Seascapes in Sharp Focus, by Lin Seslar $24.95 (cloth)

Painting with Acrylics, by Jenny Rodwell $19.95 (cloth)

Painting with Pastels, edited by Peter D. Johnson $15.95 (paper)

Pastel Painting Techniques, by Guy Rddon $23.95 (cloth)

The Pencil, by Paul Calle $16.95 (paper)

Perspective in Art, by Michael Woods $12.95 (cloth)

Photographing Your Artwork, by Russell Hart $15.95 (paper)

Putting People in Your Paintings, by J. Everett Draper $22.50 (cloth)

The Techniques of Wood Sculpture, by David Orchard $14.95 (cloth)

Tonal Values: How to See Them, How to Paint Them, by Angela Gair $24.95 (cloth)

You Can Learn Lettering & Calligraphy, by Gail & Christopher Lawther $15.95 (cloth)

Oil/Art Appreciation

Encyclopaedia of Oil Painting, by Frederick Palmer $22.50 (cloth)

Controlled Painting, by Frank Covino $14.95 (paper)

Painting in Oils, edited by Michael Bowers $18.95 (cloth)

Painting with Oils, by Patricia Monahan $19.95 (cloth)

To order directly from the publisher include $2.00 postage and handling for one book, 50¢ for each additional book. Allow 30 days for delivery.

North Light Books
1507 Dana Avenue, Cincinnati, Ohio 45207
Credit card orders
Call TOLL-FREE
1-800-543-4644 (Outside Ohio)
1-800-551-0884 (Ohio only)
Prices subject to change without notice.

3693